Gallop to Freedom

Training Horses
with Our Six Golden Principles

FRÉDÉRIC PIGNON & MAGALI DELGADO

WITH DAVID WALSER

TRAFALGAR SQUARE
North Pomfret, Vermont

First published in 2009 by
Trafalgar Square Books
North Pomfret, Vermont 05053

Printed in China

Library of Congress Cataloging-in-Publication Data
Pignon, Frédéric.
  Gallop to freedom : training horses with our six golden principles/ Frédéric Pignon &
Magali Delgado ; with David Walser.
    p. cm.
  Includes index.
  ISBN 978-1-57076-420-2
  1. Show horses--Training--Canada--Quebec (Province) 2. Horse trainers--Canada--
Quebec (Province) 3. Circus performers--Canada--Quebec (Province) 4. Cavalia. I.
Delgado, Magali. II. Walser, David. III. Title.

  SF287.P54 2009
  798.2'4--dc22
                                    2009027917

Book and jacket design by Carrie Fradkin

Typefaces: Garamond, John Handy, Bickham Script, Parisian

10 9 8 7 6 5 4 3

Dedication

*To Templado and Dao
who guided us on our journey of discovery*

Contents

This book is not intended to be a biography. It is meant to provide an accurate account of the philosophy and training methods of Frédéric Pignon and Magali Delgado, husband and wife, two extraordinary horsemen with abilities and instincts few of us had ever witnessed before their appearance on the international scene in the acclaimed equine "spectacular" *Cavalia*. Because Frédéric and Magali have led such interesting lives, however, we have included stories and photos illustrating their early days, their challenges and triumphs, alongside explanations of their unique approach to horse training. (Although truthfully "training" is not what they would call it—"game-playing" probably being a better choice of words.)

Frédéric and Magali go to great lengths in this book to explain why every horse is an individual and should be treated as such, with special care and focus devoted to developing his intelligence and initiative. And it is because horses are all different that they cannot tell you exactly what to do with *your* horse, but they can, and do, tell you what *they* have done with *theirs*. The remarkable results—as seen in the breathtaking images included in this book—speak for themselves: happy, fulfilled horses performing, both on the "spectacular" stage and in the competitive dressage arena, only because they *want* to.

Preface

by David Walser

Frédéric Pignon and Magali Delgado achieved their present esteemed reputation in the horse world despite coming from an unusual direction: that of the artistic theatrics of the equine "spectacular." It is perhaps because of this that they chose a writer who is not steeped in the traditions of the equestrian industry and would not, therefore, expect to produce another "method" or manual on horsemanship. They wanted someone who would express the philosophy, the beliefs, the emotion, and the passion behind their approach. I hope that I have been able to do some justice to this wish and to pass on some of what they have learned and believe in the interest of a better world for horses.

While working on this book my discussions always took place with Frédéric and Magali together, though Frédéric more often spoke for both of them. I have used chapter 1 to introduce the two of them to you. Magali tells her own story in chapter 4 and in the remaining chapters, it is Frédéric's voice that you hear, though Magali adds many additional comments.

These two people are happily married in two senses: to each other and to their horses. Their aim is to further the understanding of how our two species communicate and to use that knowledge for the good of the horse, as much as for our own pleasure and satisfaction. They have made extraordinary discoveries along the way—and if you are among the two million or so people who have seen them perform in *Cavalia* you will be eager to share these. This is but a "snapshot" of their lives and the knowledge they have acquired so far; they hope their journey together will take them much further.

There are a few terms that appear throughout the text that readers may be unfamiliar with:

Cabrade   A movement in which the horse rears up on his hind legs as high as he is able to. Considered by some to be an expression of joy. Frédéric and Magali do not allow their horses to remain as high and for as long as they do in many circuses and horse "spectaculars" because of potential strain.

Jambette   A movement executed when the horse is standing still: he raises a foreleg, bringing it forward and upward as high as possible, often used to prepare for the Spanish walk.

Passage   A slow and highly cadenced trot, high-stepping and rhythmical, with the horse "suspended" for a moment in the air.

Pesade   The horse lifts his forehand, bends his forelegs, and balances on his hind legs with his body raised at an angle of about 45 degrees or more.

Piaffe or piaffer   A cadenced trot where the horse steps from one diagonal pair of legs to the other with a moment of suspension and appears to remain on the spot.

Poste or post   A dangerous stunt where a rider stands upright on the back of a team of horses at the gallop. The team may consist of three, four, six, or even more horses.

Reverence   The horse drops down on one front knee and extends the other leg straight out before him, dropping his head as if in a "bow."

Spanish walk   A high-stepping, expressive walk where the forelegs extend up-and-forward in an exaggerated manner.

Volte   A circular figure with a diameter of 6, 8, or 10 meters.

Voltige   A dangerous stunt where a rider holds himself upside-down either above the saddle or down one side of the horse with his head just clear of the ground, and "ricochets" with his feet from side to side of the horse while at a gallop.

Introducing
Frédéric Pignon and Magali Delgado

BY DAVID WALSER

The year is 1993 in Avignon, France, at the annual Crinières d'Or (Golden Manes) Show. The amphitheater lights dim, the music strikes up, the voices of the seven-thousand-strong audience drop to a murmur. Suddenly the arena fills with light and from one side erupts a horse such as few have seen: a brilliant white Lusitano stallion at full gallop. The crest of his powerful neck is arched above his head, his mane flies behind him and from his flanks flow brilliant red streamers. How will he stop at this speed? But before it is too late he leans into a turn and still at a breathtaking pace, circles the arena. Abruptly, he skids to a stop facing the audience but his mane, the longest anyone there has seen, continues above and in front of him until it falls in cloud of white around his hooves.

The audience breaks into ecstatic applause. The horse peers about him. He is clearly anxious. But it is not the clapping that makes him anxious: he is looking for something. He spins on his hind legs and gallops toward the exit. The spectators turn their heads to follow him and there they see the tall, motionless figure of Frédéric Pignon. As the horse reaches him Frédéric sinks onto one knee. The horse comes to a stop in front of him and immediately rears up above his head into a beautiful cabrade. The horse is the young Templado and it is his first appearance before an audience. At this moment a star is born and, at the same time, a mutual devotion is sealed that will only be broken by the death of Templado fourteen years later. There *follows a dance between man and horse that is so spontaneous, and full of excitement and joy, that those fortunate enough to be there are either applauding or crying. All too soon for them Frédéric, followed by the galloping Templado, runs at full speed toward the exit where he is met by Magali Delgado, his young wife, who is about to go on stage herself, and the other members of their troupe, all shedding tears of emotion and relief. It was a moment of revelation and elation in Frédéric's life that he and the others will never forget.*

Templado—a vision of grace at liberty.

This event turned Templado into a household name—first in France and then in Europe, Canada, and the United States. He had a brilliant career both on stage and on film. He was on the front cover of practically every major equestrian magazine. Templado's first appearance was in a sense miraculous because before he galloped into that arena he had not committed himself totally to his friend Frédéric, who had no idea what Templado would do when he came on stage. Taking the decision to open the show with Templado was risking his career since he could not have known how the horse would react to thousands of applauding people in a place he had never been to before.

Frédéric Pignon and Magali Delgado have much in common when it comes to horses. They both grew up in the country and had their own horses from an early age. They learned about horses, how to care for them, and how to ride in a completely natural way and picked up their knowledge as they went along. Neither was formally taught and they came quite separately to the conviction that all training had to take place against a background of love and trust; that any progress based on domination or fear was pointless and unacceptable.

Templado in Paris, 2002. Frédéric is in the show costume of the Royal Andalusian School of Equestrian Art. The beauty of Templado's mane always had a magical effect on crowds.

Also at an early age, they each developed a love of entertaining: they put on displays for their families and this became a passion. It led Frédéric to acquiring all the skills of a master trick-rider from the celebrated Georges Branches, which he was soon exhibiting in horse "spectaculars." It led Magali in the same direction at first: trick riding and bareback riding. Her parents owned a Lusitano horse breeding farm, so she grew up surrounded by horses who were as much a part of her life and upbringing as her parents and siblings. Dressage was always a special interest for her and at eighteen she decided to be a state-certified instructor. Then she not only began to dream of introducing

The day after, Templado shows he approves of Frédéric and Magali's wedding!

the highest standards of dressage into the world of entertainment but actually started the long battle to reduce the barriers between it and the world of dressage competition.

After a period of advanced training in Portugal Magali returned to France and taught at the equestrian center in Apt. Frédéric was hired to teach there as well. And so they met. It was not long before they discovered that they had a shared approach to understanding and dealing with horses, and the same philosophy. Within months, they had opened their own stable and were soon putting on solo performances or taking part in larger equestrian shows all over France. When a Monsieur Lapouge saw one of their acts and engaged them for the well-known *Cheval Passion* spectacular, major promoters wanted them to perform in all the biggest European venues. It was not long before they were spotted by Don Manuel

Magali and Dao in Cheval Passion in 2000. They have just finished an act called "Renes à la Ceinture" in which the reins are attached to Magali's belt while she rides tempi changes, passage, and piaffe. She then gathers them at the end of the act as Dao lowers himself to the ground.

Vidrié Goméz, one of the legendary founding riders of the Royal Andalusian School of Equestrian Art, and invited to join his team for a show in Santo Domingo, Dominican Republic, where they remained for two years.

Their comeback appearance, in Nimes at the invitation of the distinguished and famous producer of equestrian events, Maurice Galle, was a triumph and in addition to spectacular stunts, included Frédéric's liberty acts with three stallions and Magali's famous "*mirror pas de deux*," which she performed with her sister Estelle on their horses Dao and Zenete.

Meanwhile, they had been engaged by *Arabian Nights*, the largest dinner show equestrian spectacular in the US as consultant trainers, brought in three times a year over a period of three years to help improve the choreography of certain numbers, so they found themselves shuttling back and forth between the European capitals and Orlando, Florida. All this time the dream of an equestrian event that would incorporate stunts, circus acts, dressage, liberty acts, live music, and wonderful costumes began to take shape.

When Normand Latourelle, a Canadian producer renowned for producing popular events throughout the world, who had also been dreaming of a multimedia equestrian show, approached them, everything fell into place. *Cavalia* was born. Starting in a small town in Canada called Shawinigan, they went on to Toronto, Montreal, Quebec, and thence to the US where they appeared in San Francisco; Berkeley; San Diego; Santa Monica; Glendale; Irvine; Las Vegas; Seattle; Phoenix; Houston; Dallas; Washington, DC; and Boston before returning to Europe.

The first time I had the pleasure of seeing Frédéric and Magali in action was in a *Cavalia* show in Berlin, Germany. Magali's contribution was, as you can imagine, a visual delight. Without bridle or saddle, holding a simple neckband, I watched her perform half-passes, Spanish walk, tempi changes, passage, piaffe, pesade, and even lying down in a perfectly controlled way so that as the horse sank onto his side, she stepped gracefully off.

Her instructions to the horse were undetectable because there were no visible signs: she has reached such a close understanding with her horse Dao that her aids are transmitted by thought and by minuscule shifts of weight. She and Dao display such perfect balance and rhythm that, even when carrying out movements like piaffe, he appears to be doing them without effort or tension. You feel the horse could continue to piaffe forever and you rather hope he will! It is only when you know the methods by which this standard is reached that you can really appreciate her achievement.

Other great riders reach a similar level of skill and perfection but it may not have been achieved with the full and pleasurable consent of the horse. Magali's certainly has for she adheres strictly to her principles when training her horses: respect for the horse is paramount and no force is used. The horse must agree to every move and happily so.

Though I had read a lot about Magali and Frédéric's acts, nothing prepared me for the appearance of one, two, and then three free stallions—magnificent Lusitanos—erupting into the arena, galloping up to Frédéric, dropping into a "reverence" as they acknowledged the audience; circling around him in perfect line like well-trained

At home in France, Magali and Dao relax after giving a dressage demonstration to the media. Although loose in an open field, Dao chooses to stay beside her instead of galloping off as might be expected—they are enjoying each other's company.

guardsmen; charging around the whole arena and returning to him for words of encouragement and praise; raising their forehands on platforms, including the low dividing wall between the stage and the audience, then extending their legs in jambettes; rearing up in cabrades; sitting down side by side in a line; and finally, lying down one after the other and often remaining perfectly still. They all appeared to radiate pleasure in their participation.

Magali and Bandolero at Tarbes in France in 2002. This was a show that Frédéric and Magali had devised featuring live musicians, and Bandolero reacted to their presence, becoming more animated, active, and energetic in his performance.

So it continued, and I only had to go to a performance on the following day to realize that the acts varied from night to night and that they were not entirely choreographed in advance. This is because Frédéric allows the horses to choose to a certain extent what they want to do. The freedom of choice is part of his training philosophy: he is never quite sure what they are going to come up with and, of course, the performances can vary according to the mood and ability of the

Templado, Fasto, and Aetes change from a right-hand circle to a left-hand circle. Frédéric has to pass underneath their necks. This was taken at the Grand Piste de Bercy in Paris in front of a crowd of 50,000.

horses performing on that night. Frédéric has found the improvisation is important for keeping the horses in a relaxed and happy state. He has also found natural expression has a special beauty that comes across to audiences: the horses appear to exude joy in their participation.

There are "liberty" acts by other trainers but none that has this degree of freedom and I have not heard of any involving three stallions, let alone six, which you can witness in Frédéric's video *L'Histoire d'une Passion* ("a passionate pursuit"). Other liberty shows are more tightly choreographed and do not allow the horse to make sudden unscripted contributions.

By now you will be, at the very least, intrigued and eager to meet the Pignons. You will want to find out their training methods and watch them at work. If you succeed, you may at this point be in for a surprise. They make no claims to having a particular system and they offer no specific techniques. What they do offer is an approach to understanding, to keeping horses, an approach that encourages a horse to explore and develop his own intelligence, and finally to give willingly to his owner as much as he is physically and mentally able when invited to do so: he is not under an obligation and it is therefore the opposite of achieving a state of submission.

You do not have to be a brilliant rider to embark on this adventure. You may want to have the companionship of a horse and see how far you can take the ability and privilege of communicating with this splendid animal. Needless to say, if you are hoping to ride well and put your newfound knowledge into practice, Frédéric and Magali take it for granted that you already have the basics of riding: a good "seat," legs, hands, and balance—fundamental skills that allow you to achieve a standard of competence.

Magali has used her knowledge to take dressage to the very highest competitive levels, but you do not have to aspire to this in order to benefit from her advice. Frédéric is the only person who gives regular public performances with three stallions at liberty in a large arena. He encourages you to do free work with your horse "in-hand" or on foot to resolve problems, but you do not have to aim toward performing liberty acts in public, let alone with stallions.

Frédéric and Magali show you what can be achieved in their performance. They can tell you about what rewards to expect from the trust of a powerful, potentially intelligent animal that for centuries

During a break outside Los Angeles, California, between Cavalia shows, Guizo expresses his joy at getting out of the horse trailer and stretching his legs.

Frédéric and Aetes in Paris in 2001 at the end of an act.

was a key contributor to human progress, but in order to experience the joy and satisfaction of this trust and what it brings in return, you have to embark on the journey yourself. Being told about it is one thing; experiencing it, another. It goes without saying that technical mastery of a horse has brought pleasure to countless people, but Frédéric and Magali are convinced that the joy of mastery cannot be equated with the joy of achievement when an animal gives to you as much as you give to him, one in which he chooses the speed at which you travel, in which he gives freely of his abilities. And why should he do this? Because, in return, you relieve him of stress. He knows he will not be forced to do anything against his will and that you will protect him from danger and any situation that he does not understand. That is the bargain.

It is easy to forget what extraordinary creatures horses are. In a way it has been their undoing that they are so adaptable. They can and have been, over the centuries, manipulated in countless different ways. They can survive the cruelest and the kindest treatment. They can be trained to do a great variety of tasks. They have astonishing endurance. Their weakness is perhaps that they adapt too readily and are therefore too easily manipulated and exploited by man once they have been harnessed and saddled. They can even be forced into submission at liberty within an arena with the use of a whip.

What people do not appreciate is that every time a horse submits to pressure, whether subtle or overt, he is diminished. Probably the great majority of people who achieve their own ends by making their horse submit are not even aware of what they have done. It is a sad fact that a horse can be made to do many things by breaking his will. If he can be persuaded to give his assent freely and pleasurably rather than give into man's pressure or clever techniques, he is not diminished.

To most people there is no distinction between these alternatives: two horses do a perfect volte or piaffe. To the untrained eye they look the same but one horse has been brought to this point of excellence by rigorous conventional and repetitive training producing stress and tension, of which the trainer may not even be aware. The other horse has arrived at the same degree of excellence as result of pleasurable work interspersed with games and never pushed beyond endurance or even beyond what he is prepared freely to give.

Magali and Frédéric can tell the difference by observation. So could the judges in 2002 at the Grand Prix in Essen, Germany, a competition that represents the highest level of dressage, and where Magali was runner-up. They said how wonderful it was to see a horse that appeared calm and unstressed after so demanding a test. At Essen in 2004, after Magali stunned the competition for a second time, she was asked by the organizer if Frédéric could give an "at liberty" demonstration at the evening gala. Her horse, Dao, was so unstressed that Frédéric was able to bring him back into the arena for an unscheduled and unrehearsed exhibition. (This occasion is described in detail on page 80.)

Everyone is aware of a new generation of horse trainers—including so-called "whisperers"—who achieve extraordinary results with horses in a very short time and with no apparent force, and there are books with precise instructions about how to achieve these results

Magali and Edros in a dressage competition, displaying the pleasure of their close harmony during their test.

with your own horse. What is it that makes Frédéric and Magali not just another part of this group? One difficulty in answering this question is that neither of them wishes to seem critical of anyone else or to be considered as rivals. They feel they are part of horsemanship's classical tradition and never-ending development of the man-horse relationship. They do not want to be identified with any particular school of thought but to be part of the whole natural growth of equine understanding and to "lower the barriers" between different disciplines of riding.

They are, however, quite different in one respect and it is largely due to Templado, an extraordinary horse who added another dimension to their understanding, that this is so.

Both Frédéric and Magali reached the point where they considered themselves capable trainers and able to deal with more or less any horse and its problems. They had taken part in lots of equestrian events where they put on displays involving anything from high level dressage to trick riding. Then something happened that was to affect their lives: the return of the young Lusitano stallion Templado that Magali's family breeding farm had sold at the age of one. Here was a horse that did not respond to anything they knew. They were not obliged to rise to the challenge of taming him, and they could have sold him, but fortunately for Templado, and for us, they were prepared to devote years of time and patience in order to discover how to work with this amazing character.

What happened was not so much that they had to find new ways of treating this horse. It was more a change of attitude and a fundamental one—in effect, a change of direction. Instead of saying to themselves, as they had done so far, "How can I get this horse to do what I want, albeit in the kindest possible way?" they learned to ask, "What would this horse *like* to do?" Then slowly but surely they built on what the horse told them. Instead of thinking of themselves as teachers, they had to become pupils. They felt they were entering new territory, one that could only be explored by an absolute determination to put the horse on a more equal footing with themselves and to abide by an immutable set of principles, based on respect and love.

Even now, twenty years after Templado entered their lives, they cannot present you with a detailed map for travel in this territory; they are travelers themselves. But they can give guidance and instill in you the resolve to start the journey and continue it. It is as if you decided to travel around the world on horseback. It would be a constant temptation to resort to quicker means of travel but you must resolve not to do so. Your journey must unfold at a natural pace, the pace of the horse. There are no quick fixes; if you resort to them, it becomes a different sort of journey.

The approach they employ can be called "positive reinforcement" rather than "negative reinforcement." The latter consists of stopping the horse doing what he wants to do, annoying him in a way, and then complimenting and rewarding him when he does right. There is a place for this in training, says Frédéric, but the emphasis must always be on the former approach: on giving pleasure until the horse wants to be within your aura. Then you will avoid the danger of aggression. When Frédéric uses the pressure of a finger to get a horse to back up, it is so gentle that you could not say that he is annoying the horse; he is making him think perhaps that life would return to its previous state of pleasantness if the finger were not there: a subtle but an important difference.

Is it worth all this trouble, you ask? Frédéric and Magali demonstrate two ways of using the knowledge and experience they have gained from their approach to horse management. In principle, there is no reason why their approach could not be used in all other equine disciplines. In fact, you could be the first person to do so! Frédéric and Magali have chosen ones that suit them, which appear to be at either end of a spectrum: covering the precision of dressage at one end and, at the other, the "looseness" of liberty acts. They could doubtless have used their approach to conquer other types of riding, but even if they had, it is certain that liberty work and dressage would have been essential elements. Magali uses liberty work as part of her own training and Frédéric has reached a very high standard of dressage. It does not matter what you do: racing, jumping, dressage, or simply going out for a trail ride or hack. What matters is finding out how to communicate with the aim of producing a symbiotic relationship, a two-way connection between yourself and your horse.

Since retiring from *Cavalia* in 2009, Frédéric has begun to hold clinics, which people can attend with or without their horses. After only a few of these he has become even more aware of the dangers of mindless repetitive training, where someone is blindly following a method. He describes with despair in his voice how he finds horses that have been so stressed that they are numbed, "dumbed down," and turned off like a light switch; they have only one desire and that is how to get to the end of whatever is demanded of them.

Frédéric and Magali welcome any other travelers on their journey of discovery, and they hope that, if you make a contribution that adds to our understanding of this wonderful creature, you will record it for posterity and for the sake of improving the lot of all horses. Horses have been used for man's purposes for centuries; we owe it to them to see what they can give us of their own free will. If we can achieve the results that Frédéric and Magali achieve with their approach, why should we use any other? Simple answer: few people have the patience or the time. To this there is no comeback, except to say, "Poor horses, your time has yet to come."

Time is of the essence; time, patience, love, courage, sensitivity, and many other qualities have to be lavished on your horse in order to allow you to see, to understand, and finally to achieve the result you aim for. But of course, there is nothing "final" about it: the process continues without an end. A journalist once asked Frédéric, "Is there anything you don't know about horses?" to which he replied, "The contrary is the case. I have only just begun to understand." The more you learn, the more you can share your knowledge and the more influence you can have. This book aims to help you achieve a fruitful and effective partnership with your horse, a partnership that will be as much a reward to him as it is to you. You will also be part of this great adventure, learning to understand and communicate with horses in new ways. Frédéric and Magali's lack of arrogance, their conviction that you should approach this subject with humility and a willingness to learn every day, must be to us all an inspiring example.

Frédéric and Magali live modest lives, trying always to be in harmony with their surroundings. They have a deep respect for nature and try to do as little damage as possible to the world around them. In a way they resemble horses since their lives are nomadic: they travel with their entire *équipe* from city to city, returning home for respite and recovery. You might wonder what will become of man-horse communication in fifty years if their work continues. Frédéric has considered this and believes extraordinary advances are possible. He hopes that one day he may be able to merely think of an instruction such as, "Follow me" and the horse will do so. To achieve these ends

A family "picnic" at the farm in L'Isle sur Sorgue, France, at peace with their surroundings.

means endless effort both to educate ourselves as well as the horse, to deepen our powers of observation and concentration: the road to understanding and in the end the road to freedom.

Frédéric and Magali have dared to question the traditional basis of training. For man and horse to meet on a new plain, they have said, "We have to build a bridge and invent a new language." A truly loving relationship between two humans requires mutual desire. Each is a privileged being for the other. Each asks the other: "Will you become my special one?" What happens though if one is a man and the other a horse? With such a chasm between them, with different intelligence, different needs, a different way of life, how can they find harmony without one dominating the other? It is this problem to which Frédéric and Magali have addressed themselves. They are in an ocean of unknowing not unlike the first explorers to cross the Atlantic. They have rejected much existing horse knowledge. They have set out to show that love can find a new way, not unlike that of a parent for a child.

The horse becomes the child whom the man helps to raise, to mature, and to learn to be free. The relationship is so intense that it

End of the day in Malibu, California, after a performance of Cavalia. A reward for everyone!

hardly leaves room for anything else. The horse is in a sense the master. The man asks to be let into the horse's world, where he goes forward with timid steps until they begin the dance together. The horse does not belong to the man but to "freedom." Frédéric and Magali are not the masters of their horses; as they tell you on the pages that follow in their own words, they are their friends and guides. Roles are reversed: the horse whispers in their ears. He becomes "the Whisperer."

Horses Then and Now

2

It is the end of an autumn day in the 1940s. My grandfather, Raymond Pignon, and his two plow horses have been turning over the stubble after the harvest. It has been a long day in the sun and all are tired, but on the last furrow the soil curves over in an almost perfect line as they come down the edge of the long field. The plow is attached to shafts running back from a strong wide leather collar but there is no bit in the horses' mouth, just a halter around their neck. A familiar call from their master turns them to the left or right, helped perhaps by a hand, laid gently on the rump of the lead horse. Other calls set them going, halt or back them up, speed them or slow them down. The horse knows what is required through familiar sounds, words and a touch with a stick or the hand in the right place. When the plow has been unhitched, my grandfather walks slowly back to his farmstead, the horses walking freely behind him, no doubt stopping to munch some grass along the way.

This same scene could have been witnessed in almost any country for hundreds of years before tractors finally replaced the last working horses and brought to a close a tradition that carried with it a body of knowledge, handed down by word of mouth from generation to generation. No one taught my grandfather to ride or to plow. He learned to communicate with the horses by watching his own father as he walked alongside him. He would learn to read how the horse felt: Was he thirsty or had he worked enough for the day? If he were overworked might he not be able to do less on the morrow?

There were of course other scenarios that would have been familiar for centuries all over the world. When the smoke cleared after a battle, right up until the nineteenth century there might have been as many dead horses lying on the field of battle as there were dead soldiers. Horsemanship was largely developed through military use and many of the problems we have today are because of the attitude to horses that stems from this tradition. Riding skills had to be quickly taught, effective for the maximum number of people, uniform in application, and took little account of the feelings of the horse. The suffering of horses over the ages, as a result of being used in this way, must be obvious to anyone, but there is a brighter side to the story: The partnership afforded man the opportunity and the privilege of establishing a relationship for work or pleasure with a large, powerful, intelligent, and useful animal.

There have surely been many ways in which man has "bent the horse to his will" but this expression, and others like "breaking-in," suggest that on the whole, his aim has been to dominate the stronger animal and that in achieving this aim he has used coercion, often ferocious and cruel. Of course, there have also been untold numbers of partnerships between man and horse where domination and cruelty were not used. When farmers all over the world depended on horses for husbandry, communication between man and horse was often at a profound level. There were possibly as many relationships based on trust and kindness as on exploitation and cruelty.

There are also stories of people whose ability to communicate with horses caused such alarm amongst the authorities, either Church or State, that they were persecuted and even burned at the stake, as in Arles in the Middle Ages. There are also famous and well-documented cases of extraordinary relationships between man and horse, of which Alexander the Great and his horse Bucephalus is one of the best known. So much of this slowly acquired knowledge was suddenly lost in a very short time because no one had thought it necessary to write it down.

In the last century advances have been made in communication that would have delighted Jules Verne: the fax and now email and the Internet have followed the telephone. Before these were invented and "proven" most people would have laughed at them; we tend only to believe what is scientifically provable.

In medicine for instance, there is a constant battle between the so-called conventional and alternative methods but every so often a cure, long accepted by an alternative practice, is suddenly "discovered," proven scientifically, and taken into the embrace of conventional medicine. It is understandable that this approach has been adopted in order to safeguard people from dangerous or ridiculous cures but there is a serious downside: areas of vital importance, such as communication between a human and an animal that cannot easily be subjected to scientific proof, are not even a subject of interest to most people, let alone to controlled research.

It may even be the case that these advances in communication, such as the Internet, have made us more arrogant about our achievements and even less eager to explore ways that offer little hope of scientific verification. Why waste our precious time? Why should we bother when we can contact someone on the other side of the world in a flash?

The answer is that we cannot use any of these new means of communication either with horses or indeed with any animal. Animals are becoming extinct every year. In 2007, the Chinese Yangtze River Dolphin, the only remaining fresh-water dolphin, joined this sad list. It is the first recorded extinction of a cetacean species—that is, a whole group or family of animals. We cannot quantify the seriousness of each new loss of an individual species, let alone a family or genus of great intelligence, but surely everyone must see that if we destroy all the animals on the land and in the oceans, man is not likely to survive. Once you acknowledge that we depend on animals for our own survival, we have a positive duty to explore the little known region of communication with these, our fellow creatures.

THE NATURE OF THE HORSE

Flight Animal

It is time to have a look at what we know about the nature of the horse. The most important thing to acknowledge is that he is a "flight animal." His natural reaction to anything that is not understood or appears to be a threat is to flee. Some animals use their strength to attack, to bite or strike; a stallion may use these methods when competing for dominance with another stallion, and a horse can strike out or bite a man, but on the whole the horse uses his enormous strength to get away from the scene of perceived danger as fast as he can. As anyone knows who has had anything to do with horses, they can be quite as startled and want to gallop off because a paper bag flies about in the wind as we imagine they might if a tiger leaped out of the bushes. Horses use speed to escape danger. In the modern world horses are almost always "contained" within a stall, a loosebox, a ring, a paddock, or at most a field, but even within a restricted space, they do not easily lose their instinct for flight when frightened.

Given that the horse has adapted to man's demands in so many ways it seems that the instinct to gallop away from danger is still central to his nature. It is my aim is to become that safe haven to which the horse instinctively turns, or returns to, when nature has goaded him to flight. Hours and days of working together will reduce the number of times the horse loses control, even for an instant, and tries to run away. There are methods by which we can introduce the horse to all sorts of new objects and experiences until it is perhaps a rare event that the horse will be surprised and flee, but this instinct will not disappear completely.

Herd Animal

A horse is also a "herd animal." In the ever-diminishing areas of the world where wild horses still live in their natural state, they do not live alone or with a mate but in a herd with a well-defined hierarchy and a leader, which can either be a stallion or a mare, and is very often an older mare. In the wild state a horse's life might consist of foraging, raising young, following the leader, or being followed in the role of leader and fleeing danger, whenever it appears. The natural habitat of the horse is the wide-open prairie or moorland and there is less of it every year that passes.

The horse has adapted incredibly well to man's way of life and to man's demands. Is it not perhaps time for man to recognize what has been taken from the horse and to look to what we might do in return? As humans, we have forced the horse to adapt to our wishes;

might we adapt to his needs and wishes? Our lives should be devoted to discovering how we can achieve this and at the same time achieve our own ends, as long as they are reasonable. Another way of putting it is that we should try to make our aims, his aims and his, ours.

We cannot give him back his wide-open prairies to gallop across; we have provided him with stabling and allowed him to spend his time in pastures either on his own or with a few companions. We have on the whole protected him from life-threatening dangers, but we should consider: Is this enough? I am convinced that it is not.

Magali's parents' breeding farm. They have an 18 hectare field (about 45 acres) with around 50 mares and foals in it together. Here the horses are returning in the evening after a good day's grazing.

Nothing could replace what the horse has lost but if we were to learn to treat horses with due respect, we would at least make a step in the right direction. Showing respect means removing the use of coercion from our dealings with them for this is the principal cause of stress. To do this we have to understand them better than we do at present. Learning to ride should start with being taught how to treat the horse and how to read his needs before we learn how to apply the leg, hold the reins, and adopt a good seat.

Who Becomes the Leader?

In a herd of wild horses, one horse becomes the acknowledged leader, often without having to fight his way up the hierarchy. How does this happen? Is it the same process by which a group of humans in a threatening situation chooses one person to lead them? Among humans it is not necessarily the physically strongest or the tallest who is chosen. Neither Napoleon, nor Hitler, nor Admiral Nelson, nor indeed Mother Teresa were imposing physical specimens but they undoubtedly had extraordinary abilities as well as charisma, and they used these for good or for ill. It is not the wisest and the best person or the one with commonsense who always becomes the accepted leader; in the world of horses the leader will not necessarily be the best physical specimen, nor the largest or fastest, which you might think reasonable considering that the horse is a flight animal. No, it is perhaps the one who in some way radiates inner strength, an intangible collection of qualities that includes confidence, experience, courage, magnetism and will power. I say "perhaps" because these are all terms developed to describe human behavior and we have to be careful when using them to describe other species.

In the world of humans, people selected as leaders often become arrogant and abuse the trust that has been placed in them; I

Gracil and Guizo are close friends who are stabled next to each other; here they do a bit of mutual grooming. Scratching another horse's back and wither is a mark of affection. Then, the storm after the calm! A moment of aggressivity between friends. Games between stallions can easily get out of hand. Frédéric stopped them after this shot was taken to avoid possible harm.

...moso and Amoroso share a tender moment between special friends, and Dao and Famoso offer each other soft bites—in this ...se, not aggressive.

...oebus and Paulus have played together since they were babies and they set their own limits—usually! It can be hard to tell them ...art when they are exchanging ideas.

suspect that this sort of arrogance does not have a parallel in the world of horses who are concentrated simply on maintaining their position until another horse develops into a stronger character, challenges them and takes over the lead.

Even if we were able to discover all the signals by which a horse exerts his will on other horses, we are not horses and therefore cannot expect to be able to copy them exactly. However, if your object is to become the lead horse you have to develop signals or body language that will be clearly understood.

A lot can be learned by observing the interaction of horses in groups or, even better, in the wild and this has been an important part of my own education. Sometimes when I watch horses in a natural environment I try imitating their signals. If it works I can say I am on the right track, but when it doesn't, I try something else. If no physical body language seems to have the right effect I might reckon that there is more to the process than external body language. So I start concentrating my thoughts and trying with every fiber of my being to tell the horse what I am also saying with my body and to listen to what he is telling me. At some point I begin to get results. It is really only a matter of commonsense.

MAN IS THE "DECIDER"

In our world, which is an artificial one for the horse, the horse needs to be given boundaries. When he is brought up in a herd, a horse learns

Frédéric and Templado in 2003. Unlike any other horse Frédéric has worked with, once Templado accepted him as a friend, he never tested Frédéric or pushed the boundaries. Their respect for each other resulted in a rare, natural balance that made rules unnecessary.

social behavior and rules from other horses. In this case I am only continuing the process when I take over. He has to integrate what I teach him so the rules must be simple, precise, and coherent. A horse living a secure life is less stressed than the horse in the wild who is responsible for himself. Instead of substituting a new form of stress, as an "enforcer," we should take on the role of "decider," not the one who imposes his will and dominates the horse. We must also keep it constantly on our minds that rules vary according to each horse. For example, my Friesian horses, Phoebus and Paulus, I can push gently away without damaging their trust; Lancelot, a Lusitano, I cannot so I have to get around the problem in another way.

Our Responsibility as Leader

When a horse in the wild takes on the role of leader, he or she assumes the responsibility of protecting those who have accepted his leadership. When we take on the role of human leader, or "decider," the term Magali and I prefer to use, we necessarily take on a greater area of responsibility than that of a lead horse in the wild. "To whom much is given" as the saying goes, "much is expected." The responsibility is not to be taken lightly; indeed, if we are privileged enough to be accepted as the human leader, without using force or any form of cruelty, it is an honor that should be cherished. When things go wrong as a result of assuming this role it is not enough to say, "I didn't know."

Lancelot in 2005. He was five years old here and had just arrived in the US, needing to learn everything from scratch. He's a very sensitive horse who needs a lot of reassurance.

Safe from Danger?

When humans think they are totally safe from threat or danger they tend to go their own way and this often leads to selfish actions because they stop being aware that every one of their actions affects other people and, ultimately, the whole world. When danger lurks and people lose faith in the security of their money or their door locks, they either turn to someone to get them out of the situation or become that person themselves.

Horses are never misled like humans into believing that they are completely safe from all danger. They always seek someone to whom they can turn in a strange or threatening situation. Even Templado, who was a natural leader, would turn to me for help and protection if faced with something he did not understand. And herein lies a reason, possibly the most important reason, why we can persuade a horse to give us his trust and possibly his devotion: a horse seeks freedom from fear and stress above all else; sugar lumps and carrots are not a sufficient substitute. If we provide this feeling of security, he will freely give himself to us.

A Step toward Respect

It is an interesting thought that humans usually seem to need a recognized common threat in order to stop selfish behavior. It is a commonplace to say that the suffering during wartime often brings out the best in people: generosity, kindness, self-sacrifice, and even frugality because food is usually in short supply. It is not as though we lack common threats to our world. The problem is for enough people to recognize them and to take action. Climate change should be enough to alert us all to the need for common action but the threat to animal species is not only related to climate change but treads closely on its heels. Learning the language of horses and using it to promote responsible communication between us and them can be a step toward treating other species with more respect, a step toward educating human beings to better appreciate the role of animals in the cycle of life and in the survival of the planet.

In human relationships there is no exact parallel to that of man and horse, but the one between a parent and an offspring is in some respects the closest. I would have to add that I am imagining a good parent! As a good parent will always be prepared to learn from the child, so we must always be ready to learn from the horse. A good parent will be to the child like a safe haven but will not want the child to remain in port all his life. A good parent will respect the child and, in turn, hope to earn the respect of the child. So it is with the horse, only we do not have the ability to communicate by word of mouth. We, of course, can use words and tones of voice but the horse cannot. This is no doubt the reason why man has so easily resorted to enforcement in his dealings with horses rather than meeting the challenge of learning their language.

Imagination, Concentration, and "Getting the Message"

Children do not normally put up barriers to imaginative ideas. If you were to say to a little child, "Today we're going to picnic on the moon," he might accept it without demur. A horse is not unlike that, but when it comes to human beings intellectual caution takes over as we grow older. Unless we are careful this goes so far that imagination is stifled. I find that in most people imagination is an underdeveloped faculty.

Before television was invented, if you had told people that one day you would be able to watch and hear people speaking in another country they might have taken you for a madman. If I say I believe that one day I will be able to project my thoughts into another person's head or even onto a screen, I would certainly be considered unusual. But the first of these we already do all the time. And as far as the second is concerned, there is a long way to go before we know how to use this ability in a controlled and reliable way but the examples of thought transference over distances, short to long, are too many to ignore. Magali and I often receive the same message from one of our horses at exactly the same moment and this ability increases as the years go by. When Templado had stopped performing in our shows we still took him with us so that we could see him every day. This worked well until one day Magali and I both received the same message from him at the same moment: he wanted to go home.

We also know that when we are working with a horse we achieve results by concentrating our minds on a certain action. Likewise, we know that if we do not concentrate, the intended action either does

On their days off from Cavalia when touring California, which were Mondays, Frédéric and Magali took the horses to Paradise Cove in Malibu. You can see Fasto is a little anxious about being alone and looking for company. His attitude, his nose and ears and eyes all tell you this. Finding Frédéric, he is happy again. They play together like two kids.

Templado catches up with Frédéric and expresses his joy. Then, he spots his brother Fasto, his inseparable friend. Here, they enjoy being together.

not take place or goes wrong. A horse seems to know whether our minds are concentrated on what we are asking him to do; it is one of the gifts that a horse makes to us: he drives home the importance of concentration. Everyone has had similar experiences in other fields but may not have had a horse to help make the connection.

Stallions Need Special Consideration

Magali says, "Stallions are not different animals from geldings but they do usually have heightened characteristics that make them a greater challenge. Being such a powerful animal they are potentially more dangerous. In my experience they become dangerous when there is too much unresolved stress, so my job is to lower the stress level and if

Contact between faces comforts Mandarin and signifies things are good between him and Frédéric. It is the same with two horses who feel good together.

On Paradise Cove in Malibu, California, Frédéric treats Fasto to some scratching and petting after a good game.

possible to eliminate it. In the wild they need to be aggressive to protect their herd so they are always more stressed than the rest of the animals. In our world they have no need for aggression, so it is our job to get rid of it. People are amazed when they see me followed by a loose stallion— and one who is showing no animosity to the stallions around him. It is the same for Fred. I once entered an arena on a stallion without saddle or bridle when there were other stallions and mares standing around. My horse showed absolutely no aggression toward the others but many people were horrified at what they considered an unthinkable risk.

"Stallions have a heightened sense of fairness so, when I am working with stallions, I have to be particularly careful not to cross the borderline of what they think is fair. If I do, I have to pull back immediately and either go for a walk or indulge the horse in his favorite game. And, when I return to the work I will try a different approach."

I agree with Magali. It is impossible to force a stallion at liberty to do anything to which he does not give his consent so I have to be particularly careful: gaining the horse's confidence and trust is the only way forward. If a stallion shows signs of fear or stress during a show, I have to deal with it on the spot. I often place my mouth against his nose or ears, just as a mare does with an agitated foal. Of course, things are different with each stallion: Lancelot regularly has moments of insecurity during a performance and when I see the signs I go up to him. If he puts his nose in my hands, it means that he still feels that way. Sometimes he gets in such a state he comes over to me and asks for help.

When Guizo is stressed he has difficulty resolving it in any other way than by conflict. I have to stop what I am doing, concentrate my mind on relaxing him, as well as massaging his favorite spots, like his gums or his withers. As with a person, he holds his breath when stressed so I have to go on until he releases his breath and, therefore, his tension.

This may make stress seem a simple matter to deal with but it is often not so easy. To eliminate fear and stress, the stallions have to accept and obey simple rules: "Do not bite me. Do not bite your neighbor." All the factors that describe our approach to horse training decide whether or not horses obey these rules and, if they do, whether it is willingly. There is no "forcing" and they know they have the right to disobey should we break our side of the bargain. Often, you can suggest one thing to a young stallion and he does another, just like a child. Sometimes you agree but it is always a matter of bargaining.

Magali finds that young stallions love "talking" to you. It is sad that so many stallions and horses in general give up trying to talk to people when they discover they are not understood. She and I encourage them and most become eager communicators. Mandarin is a wonderful case in point: he even makes a special noise if, for example, he doesn't like a new exercise. When she is working with him and he complains she will leave off and return later. When he decides it is not so hard after all, he makes a different, milder noise. When he finally agrees, he does it without complaint. At this point he will often make a soft whinnying sound.

WHAT DO HORSES THINK ABOUT US?

It is not easy to know the answer to this question since there are no exact comparisons in their life. I am not a predator like the wolf. Nor am I an alpha horse who would, in the wild, rule by fear and create stress. I feel that my parent-child description is possibly the closest parallel. But how do we then integrate the horse into our world in the most balanced way? Gone are the wide-open spaces; the horse is obliged to live in our constricted world. Man spreads his tentacles across the earth, covering it in concrete, cutting down trees, and invading the remaining wilderness. In order for the horse to survive he has to live with us and we are therefore forcing on him a life that is essentially alien to him.

What then are the most important requirements for the horse to be contented? Like us, horses appreciate freedom and also like us, they like their own space. Both these can be satisfied by a field where they can be let out from time to time and a pleasant stall, loose box, or stable of the right proportions. Our gift to the horse is to relieve him of stress; his gift to us, if we allow it, is a lesson in communication, not

Templado grazing at home in France after he told Frédéric and Magali that he no longer wanted to be on tour. Frédéric and Magali traveled home to be with him once a month, whenever there was a break in performances.

only between man and beast but between man and man. The longer I live in the company of horses the more I feel my ability to communicate with other humans deepens and the more I appreciate the need for respect, not to judge too easily, to be tolerant, to have compassion and acceptance. That is the horse's gift to me.

Part of the herd from Magali's parents' stud. Frédéric and Magali spend many hours watching the interaction of the horses in the herd, observing their maneuvers within the hierarchy, and the way in which they play before and after the pecking order is established.

DO HORSES HAVE A SENSE OF HUMOR?

It is always risky to use words invented to describe human characteristics but horses certainly have something very close, perhaps more of
a sense of fun. Magali tells how, in Madrid, she was showing Phoebus
off to members of the press from the next venue we were going to: "As
you can imagine, we always have to get advance publicity before moving on to a new city. I had been talking for some time—perhaps a little
too long for Phoebus not to be the center of attention—when he suddenly darted off across the arena and fetched the rope that I had used
to lead him into the arena. He came up to me and pushed it forcefully
into my hand, as if to say, 'Enough is enough!'

"On another occasion, I was sitting on Gracioso talking to
journalists while Frédéric was in the arena working with Phoebus. At
some point Fred had to deal with something else so Phoebus was left
to wander about on his own. I happened to glance at him and knew
immediately that he was up to something. I saw him pick up Fred's whip
that was lying on a bench and amble over toward me. Now Gracioso
is like a machine when it comes to piaffe: you only have to touch his
back and he goes into one like clockwork. Phoebus happened to do
this by accident: it worked perfectly so he continued and Gracioso and
I went on with piaffe—much to the amusement of everyone except
perhaps me. In fact I could not stop the piaffe as long as Phoebus was
behind me! It was only after some time that I was able to attract Fred's
attention and get rescued."

Frédéric Pignon: My Life With Horses

3

MY FORMATIVE YEARS

Strangely enough, Magali and I had parallel childhoods, only 200 kilometers (125 miles or so) apart in France: Magali in Cavaillon and me in Bonlieu dans la Drôme. Our earliest memories involve horses. My father had been brought up on a farm and although he had become a school teacher by the time I was born, he constantly spoke of his love of horses and everything about them. I even remember him saying that he loved the pungent aroma of fresh still-warm horse manure!

When I harnessed our dog to a small cart I thought of him as a horse. I dreamed of horses and when I was seven, my father gave up teaching and bought a farm. Suddenly, there were real horses and our dog and cats and poultry and even a tame ewe for company. If I slept late the ewe would come into my room in the morning to wake me. I rode to school on my own pony, Belle, and left her in an adjacent field during the day. I could hardly wait to get back home and join the animals.

I wanted to be a stunt rider and from an early age. I and my brother Jean-Francois, who also had his little mare Gazelle, devised horse shows for our parents and friends. I felt more at ease with my horses than with people and became absorbed with the possibilities and mysteries of communication with animals. I remember putting my head against the horses' head to see if I could experience some transfer

Frédéric, age eleven, with Frimousse, already showing his natural communication skills.

of thoughts. I watched cats, birds, and dogs to try and understand how they communicated with their own kind and with other species.

Jean-Francois and I both went to a stunt school, La Mer du Sable in Paris, where we were taught by Georges Branche. We learned all the usual stunts including trick riding, jumping from great heights, and so on and this was an important part of my development and my riding skills.

However, as I was also interested in drawing and music I decided to go to Les Beaux Arts in Valence. I lasted two years before realizing that the rather artificial life of an art student was not for me and returned full time to a life centered around horses. The time at art school was not wasted because my interest in art and music continues and the horse "spectaculars" I develop combine these essential artistic elements: music from different cultures and costumes that enhance the effect of the spectacle and draw a response from the horses. I have also continued drawing and some of my drawings have been used to illustrate children's books.

COMMUNICATING WITH HORSES

My education in learning about the mysteries of horse communication continues with every new day. As I become better at it I find that I am

In 1989 Frédéric finished training as a stunt rider in Mer de Sable near Paris, before returning to Apt, near where he lived. Here is a sequence of movie frames with Frédéric performing stunts on Hortelano, a son of Perdigon, one of Magali's horses.

gradually reducing my body movements and increasingly relying on the power of thought. Over the years I have met and worked with some extraordinary riders and trainers and there is no doubt that they have influenced me in this. However, I have always felt it essential to develop my own approach and not to accept unquestioningly the experience and convictions of others.

MAJOR INFLUENCES

Among the "horse people" who have influenced me the most, I would list Don Manuel Vidrié Gómez, Corky Randall, Linda Tellington-Jones, my family (which includes my father, Magali, and her family), and last but not least, Templado.

Don Manuel Vidrié Gómez

Don Manuel, the famous Spanish breeder and trainer at the Royal Andalusian School of Equestrian Art, is one of the top horse trainers in Spain. He has a profound knowledge of horses and of training in the classical mode. He has a similarly profound knowledge of bulls since he selected those used in the *corridas* for years: he learned to judge the actions of a bull to see if it was suitable for the bull ring, just as he learned to choose and train horses. A bullfighter, if he wants to stay alive, has to be able to read and anticipate the animal's actions.

When we first met Don Manuel was creating an equestrian spectacular that he planned to take to Santo Domingo in the Dominican Republic. A young rider, hoping to work for Don Manuel, approached us to see if we could give him some training. When he heard about us Don Manuel was intrigued enough to send a scout to visit, and as a result of the scout's report, he asked if he could come to see us himself at our stables and our home in France.

You have to picture us at the time: we had not yet made very much money, we lived in a mobile home and we were generally considered a bit odd. He, on the other hand, had a well-established reputation and was revered in Spanish and even European horse circles. We were really shy about meeting him but from the moment he arrived he radiated enthusiasm and put us at ease. He came on a day when we had almost a foot of fresh snow; he loved our place and everything we showed him, and insisted on being given a little impromptu performance.

I opened a stall and out came Templado, who adored snow, following me like a puppy. There were several exits from our yard with no gates and Don Manuel immediately became anxious about the horse escaping. I reassured him and began to play a few games with Templado who looked at his best, galloping about in the snow with his long mane flying, ending in a "reverence" toward the great man. Then Magali gave a demonstration of some high level dressage movements without bridle or saddle. He seemed overcome and said, "You and your horses must come with me to the Caribbean where I am going for a couple of years to put on a show in Santo Domingo. I shall go away for an hour and come back with a contract. You must decide by then."

Though we had little idea of the whereabouts of the Dominican Republic, we decided to grasp the opportunity, so Magali and I, with our eight horses and the pony, embarked for the other side of the world. First though, we spent three months in Spain as guests at Don Manuel's hacienda while we learned the ropes. To show you how considerate he was, the day we arrived in Spain we saw that he used straw for bedding in his stables. This made us rather anxious because our horses were used to wood shavings and we were afraid they would eat the straw. We

Frédéric and Magali celebrating her birthday in Segovia, Spain, ten years after they first met. Here, they are joined by two people they adore: Don Manuel Vidrié Gómez and his wife, Isabelle.

At Don Manuel's bidding, Frédéric and Magali took their family of horses to Santo Domingo for two "dream years." Here they are on Dao and Aetes, and wearing traditional Spanish costumes.

voiced our fears to Don Manuel and within half an hour all the stalls for our horses had been made over with wood shavings.

We worked with him every day, absorbing his knowledge and experience. He taught us the importance of endless patience and to work without producing any stress in the horse. Even from a distance he could see exactly where the horse was looking; no doubt he had learned this skill working with bulls, as his life depended on knowing that the direction of the eyes dictates the direction in which the animal goes—if its attention is drawn to one side it tends to turn that way. Both bulls and horses have such a large field of vision they only have to move their eyes a little bit to look in a different direction, and since there is much less white visible around their pupil than in a human eye, they are more difficult to "read." Sometimes the ears help to give you an indication, too.

Every action of Don Manuel's was finely controlled and precise, and he seemed to be able to achieve exactly what he wanted. He was particularly concerned with how to "engage" the rear end of the horse, as well as the need to achieve perfect balance. He would work for hours on the Spanish walk without showing any impatience as so many trainers tend to, and without losing the interest and attention of the horse. Again, unlike most trainers, he did not use the whip as means of aggression: he would use it to "tickle" or barely touch a spot on the horse and then congratulate the horse when he got a reaction.

When Don Manuel didn't agree with something that I did, instead of saying, "You mustn't do this," he would suggest, "Why don't you try that?" Though he had never seen any liberty work with horses before meeting us, he was fascinated by what I was doing; he was able to understand it immediately and to give me help and advice. He exuded quiet strength and confidence; it was a privilege to work for someone of that caliber.

Amusingly, he fell in love with our dog, Bulle, and the love affair seemed to be mutual. He took Bulle in the car with him everywhere and even into bars and restaurants. Normally Spanish owners of such places are not keen on dogs entering their establishments but Don Manuel was such a famous and respected person that he could get away with anything!

One day, Don Alvaro Domecq Romero—the famous *rejoneador* and director of the Royal Andalusian School who was a friend of Don

Manuel's and the acknowledged master of classical dressage—came to watch Magali and me put on a display, concocted especially for him. We could see him sitting impassively and motionless behind the glass screen in the arena with his chin resting on his hand and we began to fear that he did not approve of what he saw. He said nothing until we had finished our numbers and then simply strode out and embraced us!

During those two years with Don Manuel our horses all reached a much higher level of training, and after our return home from the Caribbean, our career in Europe really took off.

Corky Randall

Corky Randall, who sadly died in 2009 after a long struggle with cancer, was perhaps the most famous ever trainer of horses for the big and small screen, and managed many memorable liberty scenes in films. Some years before traveling to the US we had seen his film, *The Black Stallion*, directed by Francis Ford Coppola, and his effective techniques and beautiful way of controlling horses at liberty had been a great inspiration to us.

I worked with Corky over a period of three months in Orlando, Florida, where he was in charge of training the horses for the dinner show *Arabian Nights*. Due to injuries he had sustained, he was unable to ride at the time and because I spoke so little English and he no French, our communication was almost entirely non-verbal. Even though we could hardly understand each other in normal conversation, when it came to working together on the horses we really had no problem at all. We worked for entire mornings in silence punctuated by "Yep!' "Oops!" and "Good reaction!" When he did not approve of something, he would make a small inclination of the head.

He taught me to become very important in the horse's world and in order to do that I had to put out a great deal of energy and be able to modify it all the time. Corky's principles included adapting himself to each horse and asking the horse to give no more and no less than he was capable of, and not to judge one horse against another. He knew how to catch and hold the horse's attention with a word or a little touch. He drove home the importance of the horse's eye: where was the horse looking? If he stopped looking at you, you had to recapture his attention.

Corky was a man of great charisma, humility, and wisdom, and his calmness and the precision of his gestures were a wonderful example to me. He never taught me "literally" but over a period of three months he shared everything he could in the most generous way. As with Don Manuel, he had a highly developed ability to "read" a horse and to know if he had the horse's attention. Every trainer has his or her own method of keeping the horse's attention but, as every trainer must surely agree, you have to keep it, and he put tremendous emphasis on doing so. Like so many good trainers he believed that horses must not be rushed.

A very special evening with Corky Randall and a friend at their first meeting with him since they all worked together on Arabian Nights in Orlando, Florida. This was the first time Corky had seen their new spectacular.

In 2000, wearing Spanish costumes at Arabian Nights—the largest dinner show in the world, owned by Galen and Mark Miller.

During this period, I realized later, I had slightly abandoned my principles by adopting a technique that achieved very quick—indeed, too quick—results. I had momentarily overlooked the paramount importance of my relationship with the horse, but afterward, when I had absorbed what I learned from Corky and had time to reflect, I saw that if a horse is persuaded to do something too quickly then he has insufficient time to decide if you are his friend or not. I returned to my more measured and more instinctive approach. I found that I could not adopt even his ideas without adapting them to my own. I have also noticed that horse trainers who claim to be using his methods are often but a pale imitation of him. We all have to find our own way but at the same time not close our minds to advances and discoveries made by other trainers.

I remember that at about the time I was working with Corky, I was asked to help with a horse, a little Arabian stallion being used in *Arabian Nights*. The horse worked well but was giving no end of trouble by galloping away every so often. The trainer was becoming increasingly impatient with him but to no effect. Could I do anything to help? I was very much put on the spot. Then I hit on an idea: when the little horse galloped away I ran after him as fast as I could. When he slowed down I ran straight past him and went on running. After a time he stopped and looked at me, obviously rather surprised. Until this moment he had thought that it was his idea to run away and, by running after him and then past him, I introduced the idea that it was a game we were both engaged in and that I, not he, had come up with the idea of running away.

From another angle, I was telling him that he had a right to run away since it was part of the game. He soon saw that it was indeed a game and came galloping after me. We continued running round each other and I went on with the game until he felt he had had more than enough and wanted to stop. By doing this I had made his will, my will; we had joined forces instead of being in opposition. We were playing together and after a few repeats, he was cured of his habit.

Linda Tellington-Jones

We first met Linda Tellington-Jones when we took part in an *Equitana* show in Essen, Germany. She was demonstrating her famous Tellington Method®, a revolutionary way of changing a horse's behavior by reducing stress and promoting a relaxed attitude. I knew about Linda from her very useful book *Getting in TTouch with Your Horse*, which explains how to analyze a horse's personality by observing his physical traits and characteristics.

There were masses of famous people from the horse world but the only person who came to see us was Linda. We felt honored as we knew what a well-respected position she held. From the first moment we met, there was a rapport, and since that meeting she has been kindness personified and given us every support. I told her about a problem I had with Fasto who was suffering from stress and she immediately offered to help. I watched her as she entered the stable and not without some trepidation when she said she was going to massage Fasto's ears. I knew he did not like people touching them, especially a stranger, but as she began gently at the base of his ears he lowered his head and a look of bliss came into his eyes. I knew I was in the presence of a special person.

On another occasion, after being shown all our horses, she pointed to Gracil. "That's the one that needs help," she said and she was right. I had not told her but Gracil had recently been causing trouble more than any other horse. Linda's work had an immediate beneficial effect and the next day Gracil was a different horse. To read about Linda's methods is helpful; to see her using her Tellington Method with her whole being concentrated on the action of her hands and giving out a flow of positive energy is mesmerizing and could not

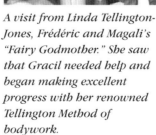

A visit from Linda Tellington-Jones, Frédéric and Magali's "Fairy Godmother." She saw that Gracil needed help and began making excellent progress with her renowned Tellington Method of bodywork.

Magali and Frédéric celebrate Linda Tellington-Jones' visit to Los Angeles in 2005. They are with their great friend Elizabeth McCall.

Frédéric's mother and father being adopted by a village dog who likes the limelight. "They were model parents," Frédéric says. "Our horses got the same education that we got."

Frédéric's father with a horse in Portugal. He believes in treating horses fairly, and he taught Frédéric to be attentive to the same principle.

be done justice in writing. Her consuming wish is to help horses. It is as if you can see the energy radiating from her.

Linda is indeed one of the people whom I have met that has an almost tangible aura of love and warmth; the horses feel it, as do humans. Since those first visits she has descended on us from time to time; we think of her as our guardian angel, or "Fairy Godmother," who drops out of the sky—usually when we most need her—bringing help and encouragement. (For a complete explanation of her work and how to do it, read *The Ultimate Horse Behavior and Training Book.*)

My Father

My father grew up on a farm and lived in a world in which the horse was part of everyday life and indeed part of the family. There were twelve children but my father was the one who looked after the horses. No one taught his father to ride and no one taught him. I remember him telling me how he first learned to make a horse trot by moving his buttocks up and down and waving his legs. My father was firmly of the opinion that the teaching of horse riding was far too conformist and with rigid techniques. He was against the military tradition of teaching and wanted children to learn naturally. I was hardly given any instruction myself, just left to get on with making my own discoveries such as flying changes at the canter.

When he gave up teaching school and returned to farming, my father already had a natural love and understanding of horses and knew how to treat them respectfully. He passed on these qualities to his children in a completely unforced way. We did not have to learn to treat animals the way we do; it was as natural as mother's milk. Even before we owned horses, Father seemed to make them a magic presence in our household and the result has been that all my siblings are passionate about them, as I am.

My uncle was also a farmer and would sometimes return from the market with three loose horses walking along behind him. He was not at all proud of this feat, which most people today would consider extraordinary and dangerous. It was just part of ordinary life with horses.

Magali

Another key influence on my understanding has been my wife Magali. I had become a good rider by the time we met, and I had taught myself several movements that I only found out later were part of haute école, or high level dressage. Magali improved my riding a lot though her competition results show she is in a league of her own when it comes to dressage. Her ability to improve a trot or piaffe, for example, without the least sign of stress or tension is second to none.

Magali not only confirmed my belief that classical dressage is the foundation of good riding but also proved to me and indeed to the world, that our approach to educating horses is capable of raising normal, "good" dressage to the absolute summit of competitive dressage, without requiring any stress-inducing techniques or abandoning our principles in the slightest degree. I can also add that, though I thought I already knew how to care for horses when we met, I found in Magali's family an even greater depth of devotion to their comfort and well-being.

In Velleron, France, in 2003, still learning to read each other.

Dao and Bandolero doing the Spanish walk in the hills of Rousillon, France, and on the same wavelength—as are their riders.

Frédéric and Magali riding Dao and Bandolero on their wedding day, and sharing the best moment of their lives so far. Magali's dress was designed by Jiki, who also designed Princess Caroline of Monaco's wedding dress. They entertained 300 guests, 30 of whom were on horseback. Frédéric wanted to make his marriage a "spectacle." The Curé had wanted to tell the story of the man who has no God being like a donkey who doesn't know where he is going, but Frédéric would not have it, because donkeys always know where they are going and the story belittled animals! At first the Curé was against the "spectacle" but came round to the idea and entered into the spirit, in the end claiming it was the best marriage ceremony he had officiated to date.

TREAT THE HORSE AS AN INDIVIDUAL

The people I have mentioned, and indeed all the people I most admire, share with me some of the same convictions and give the same advice: every horse must be treated as an individual and your approach to each must be geared to that individual. You may have the same final aim with every horse but be prepared to take a different road. You should never assume that you can use the same technique with two horses. You must first learn about the horse you are dealing with and then adapt what you already know or even break new ground by trying something you have never tried before. To do this you must observe the horse; listen to him; make the horse confident, trusting, and relaxed; and finally set the parameters of what you are doing.

An even more vitally important thing: you have to *believe*. Without losing hold on reality you have to believe that you can communicate with the horse and that one day, with persistence, you will have such close communion that you may be able to change leads at every stride with no detectable instructions, as Magali does during her performances. A huge shoal of sardines changes direction as if it were one fish. How does it do it? And since it can, why cannot we do similar things? A dog rushes up to a cat; the cat sits still and holds its ground. With a little luck, the dog stops the attack. What determines this? We are always witnessing examples of communication between different species of animals and between the same species. You must believe that you can continue to improve communication between yourself and the horse, and if everyone shares their discoveries then the day when we really understand may arrive sooner rather than later.

TEMPLADO

Templado:
"I am as free as the wind. I shine like a star but in your eyes I see only the reflection of my own transparency. You do not yet understand but I know you can. Open your mind: you will learn more about me and I about you."

Of course, the last great influence on both Magali and me was that of

Templado. Until I met him, I thought of myself as fairly knowledgeable. With Templado, I had to start again from scratch.

When Templado came back to us at the age of three after having been sold by Magali's parents when he was a yearling, he was in a dreadful state. I remember his tail and mane, all snagged with lumps of mud. He was absolutely unmanageable. Nothing could be asked of him. Any sudden movement and he would shy away. His eyes

The morning run—Templado leads by a head.

showed fury and wild fright. If anyone went past his stall he would turn nervously away. I tried taking him out on a longe line but at the slightest abrupt movement he took fright and reacted with terrifying violence. If he broke loose, as he sometimes did, it could take three hours to catch him.

This was an unexpected and strange situation for me. I rather thought I knew how to train any horse. I'd had a lot of experience with horses and had learned to communicate well with them—or so I thought—and reckoned I was able to tell them what I wanted. Without much difficulty I could persuade a young horse to go down on his knee. I had done trick riding in lots of shows and successfully performed potentially dangerous acts, but here I was presented with a horse that did not respond to anything I asked of him. It was as if all my considerable experience was for nothing.

We were not obliged to keep Templado. He was a beautiful looking creature and growing more beautiful by the week; he would have been easy to sell. Also, it was not as if we were well off. At that time we only had five working horses— Botijo and Amoroso for dressage, with Dao being trained and almost ready to perform; and Urano and Flequillo for trick riding, poste, Roman riding, and cascade—so another horse that contributed nothing to our shows and who needed time and lots of attention was a burden. At the very least, it was like having another dog in the house—not a working dog, but one who needed considerably more care than a "pet."

A photo of the young Templado: Magali and Frédéric in 1989, not long after they had met, with Fleur, a friend. They are on three sons of Perdigon—Terso, Tenerio, and Templado—all five years old, and they are preparing to take part in a parade.

No doubt some chemistry began to work soon after he arrived. It was a challenge of a new sort. We had to question and set aside our previous knowledge and try again. Templado became part of the establishment and was just allowed to "exist." We stopped making demands on him but every day we spent time watching him, trying to understand him, and trying to make contact.

There was another factor: Templado was one of the many sons of Perdigon, the leading sire at Magali's parents' stud farm. The first time I saw Magali at a *Crinières d'Or (Golden Manes)* show (wonderfully attired in an outfit that, I later learned, she had made herself) she was performing a dressage number consisting of passage, piaffe, half-passes and Spanish walk on Perdigon. By the time Magali's parents gave us Templado, many sons and daughters of Perdigon had passed through our hands so we knew the family characteristics. We mistakenly thought we were halfway to understanding Templado: he exhibited some of the same traits as his siblings and he looked like them, so maybe this was another reason why we stayed the course.

Templado Gives an Inch

One day we realized from little signs that Templado was inviting us to follow his lead but also telling us there was really no question he was going to follow ours. Once I saw this I began to change my attitude. I suppose I responded to small concessions on his part, which I would not have done had I still thought he could be persuaded to change his ways. Once I accepted the idea that anything suggesting domination by me produced in him an ungovernable fury, and made it clear that I did not even want to try, I began to make progress.

I remember the day when a most extraordinary thing happened. During a session I sank onto one knee, probably out of despair! As if it were a signal, Templado came up to me and went into a magnificent cabrade above my head. It was his game and I went along with it, abandoning all the traditional notions that the animal has to give way to the human. From then on I could get him to do a cabrade above me simply by dropping onto one knee. I was constantly on the lookout for any pleasurable idea that might cross his mind. As soon as I saw the slightest chink in his "armor" I tried to take advantage of it. It is hard to describe the feeling of excitement that Magali and I experienced as we began to make progress, even though painfully slowly.

One day I was watching Magali play with Templado as we often did. She was doing it in the most natural and unforced way and I was moved by the spontaneous pleasure they were both exhibiting. It was exactly like two people enjoying themselves, and it was probably at that moment that I thought, we must use this in our shows one day. I saw that all he had to do was be himself: to share his beauty and grace in movement, without performing any special steps. I suddenly understood how the joy of what they were expressing in their game was the essential part of it and that it was something very simple.

The Crinières d'Or Show

As the time came for this annual show—the *Golden Manes*, the top gala equestrian spectacular of its kind in France—I decided that we should propose to perform an act. Until then we had taken part in all sorts of smaller local events; this would be something in an altogether different league. I put together a proposal that would demonstrate our various skills and appeal to Pierre Lapouge, the director: an haute école dressage number and trick riding. On the front of the proposal I put one of my drawings of Templado, his magnificent mane flying out above him as he galloped along. I had not really thought anything out at this juncture, but the idea of including Templado in the show had taken root.

I went to see Monsieur Lapouge. You must understand I was a very young man and extremely nervous about the meeting. Well, M. Lapouge carefully leafed through the proposal, which a designer friend of mine had helped to prepare, and said, yes, he was interested in this mix of high level dressage and trick riding. Then he saw the picture on the front. "And I must have this," he said. "If I have this, I'll take you on." I looked M. Lapouge in the eye and said, "You shall have it."

M. Lapouge made a date on which to come and see us and by the time he arrived at our farm we had prepared our demonstration exactly as though it was in front of an audience at a show. I had made up my mind to risk everything on Templado. It was like putting one's money on a single number at roulette. It was a case of following my instincts but I admit that as the moment arrived I feared I might have thrown our chances away by gambling on a horse that still only did what he wanted to do and could be asked for nothing.

We had lights in the arena and beautiful music from the film *La Belle Histoire* to resemble proper show conditions. I opened the gate and in went Templado, immediately breaking into a gallop, looking magnificent as his long mane streamed behind him. I ran into the arena not having the least idea what he would do in the ring with these strange conditions. When Templado had galloped about for a bit he came toward me. I could tell that he was responding to the sense of occasion. He galloped round me, we played a few games together, he chased me and I, him, and when I went down onto a knee he did a magnificent cabrade above my head. Need I say that M. Lapouge was completely won over and indeed fell in love with Templado on the spot. "Where on earth did this horse spring from?" he asked me.

First Time before an Audience

By the time we performed at the *Crinières d'Or* in 1993 I was again in such a state of nerves that I almost lost my confidence. I had decided to bring Templado on first. In front of an audience of 7,000, I entered and released him into the middle of the arena. I immediately had the feeling that he was reacting well to the din of the applause, the music, and the huge audience. He reared up in a cabrade and then crossed the stage with a new high-stepping gait that I did not recognize; it was as if he had kept it for a special occasion. He galloped about, showing off his wonderful mane but suddenly stopped. He looked about anxiously, spotted me, and raced toward me. It was the key moment in our relationship: I knew that at that instant he had accepted me as his friend and safe haven, to whom he would turn in a moment of doubt. He had also demonstrated that he was a true "showman." Incidentally, the commentator, Thierry Clement, who gave the live commentary at the *Crinières d'Or* show at which Templado made his first appearance, told me fifteen years later that the memory of Templado's spectacular entry into the arena was quite simply the best visual image of all his life.

All our numbers went well but Templado was the star, and we realized that he was now *our* star, our guiding light and the key to our

Fasto and Templado sitting at the show in Essen, Germany. If Templado was "on duty," he always had to come on first, and he'd then accept that other horses joined the act—but if he was not first, woe betide! When he worked with Frédéric, Frédéric "belonged" to him in his mind. He found it disturbing to

growing reputation. He was on the posters and it was his image that led producers to buy our act. He had begun by putting all our years of experience into question; he had changed our way of thinking; he had laid the foundation to a new understanding and a new approach to horse training; he had changed the direction of our lives and gave back more than any other horse.

Templado's Development

Though this event was a key moment, it did not mark any real change in the direction or pace of our progress together. I still had to show all the respect and caution that I had learned was the only basis of working together. I could never overstep the mark or move too quickly. It was as if Templado had to agree to every move in the game. There was no question of me sitting on my laurels and telling myself that I was a great trainer. Nor did I want to do this. But there was a sea change: we were working together in a new world of discovery.

have others around and at first he would jostle them but came to accept them because Frédéric made it clear to him that he was the leader. Frédéric never had to attract Templado's attention because it was always fixed on him. You could see their symbiosis when they danced together.

Templado's problem seemed to be an almost paranoid fear of losing his independence. The slightest misunderstanding would bring on the fear; he was like a son shouting at his father, "You don't understand me!" So I tried to understand and to put myself in his skin and see myself from his point of view.

First I had to convince him that I meant him no harm and that I was not going to use any force whatsoever to get my way. I learned to observe every tiny movement of his nostrils, ears, and eyes, indeed his whole body, to work out whether he was satisfied and happy with the situation. Gradually, Magali and I both understood that only through game playing, usually games of his own choice, could he interact with us without feeling his freedom was at risk.

We were soon cooperating in discovering new games and new ways to entertain audiences as well as ourselves. I made mistakes: one evening when I was waiting to go on I bent down to pick up my stick. Templado understood the act of bending down as a signal to race away, which he immediately did, snapping the rein I was holding him with in the process. Some of these mistakes would set us back weeks but I had learned to be patient, and in his own time he would overtake the point at which he had taken fright and then put the problem behind him.

One particular incident later in Templado's life helps to throw light on the extraordinary relationship that eventually formed between us. On a long internal flight in the United States, Templado fell and became cast—jammed between the sides of his portable stall in an extremely awkward and uncomfortable position. Understandably he was in a panic. It is not out of the question to sedate a horse in such a state, and in extreme cases, a horse may be euthanized if it is feared he will damage the plane and endanger the rest of the passengers. I agonized over the fact that he might not survive the flight unless something was done.

As a horse person, I knew it was perhaps not wise to climb into a confined space with a terrified and half-collapsed stallion, but I felt I had no choice. I managed to calm Templado and he somehow knew he had to cooperate in order to survive. With an enormous physical effort on both our parts, Templado was restored to a standing position and saved.

The last photograph taken of Templado at the end of one of Cavalia's US tours—in Irvine, California, only days before going to Europe. His mane was at its longest and best, and he knew what an effect it had on people. When photographers focused on him, he knew exactly what was expected and played to the camera.

A Special Quality

Templado became a star quite suddenly. He was in all the magazines, often on the covers, and journalists were constantly coming to photograph him. The *Crinières d'Or* appearance changed his life as well as ours.

The strange thing is that I never had the impression of "training" Templado, and indeed his appeal was not that he did the classical dressage steps on demand. He could do a good piaffe, lie down, or sit, though he didn't much care for these. His genius was his exuberant showmanship that captivated audiences. Once he had decided to hand me his full trust he almost needed no training; he picked things up without difficulty and remembered them.

The qualities he gave in abundance were charisma, beauty, and energy. He arrived in the arena with presence and panache. Even at his last public appearance, after he had been so ill that the vet thought he only had a short time to live and never dreamed that he might go on stage again, Templado seemed to swell visibly as the moment drew near. His neck, from being a more or less straight line from ears to body, arched imperiously, asserting domination over all the other horses and demanding everyone's attention.

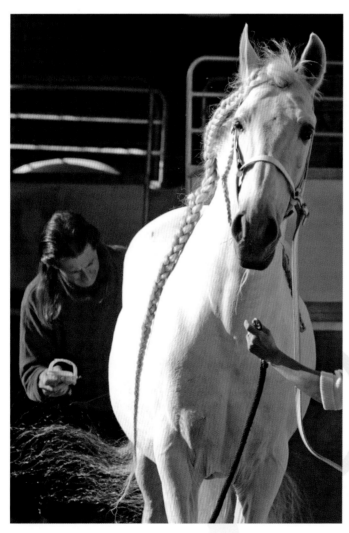

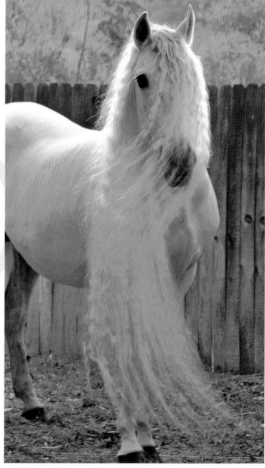

Templado had to have his mane braided every day and washed in the best shampoo once a week. He knew he had a special mane and invented a peculiar rotating motion with his neck that showed it off. He soon discovered he could please the public by throwing it about—he made the connection between the movement and the applause. Coincidentally it also helped to clear the mane out of his eyes.

At each performance he gave his all: he leaped back and forth or twisted on the spot with mesmerizing invention. He exuded energy, he galloped, he threw his mane—longer than the manes of any of his brothers—so that it described graceful swirls above him like smoke rising on a still day. He just followed my movements or I followed his; we danced by doing voltes where I turned the opposite way to him as if in a waltz. We exchanged energies like two tennis players. Needless to say these performances kept me very fit!

There was no rehearsal: sometimes his performance was good, sometimes it didn't quite come off, but usually it was brilliant and witnesses said it took their breath away as it did mine. He was beauty personified. And then, as the tresses of his mane settled from their wild dance, he sank into a "reverence" on one knee and lay or sat as still as a tombstone while he soaked up the applause of the audience.

Templado: "Now I am as free as the wind and I shine like a star. I see myself reflected in your eyes as your equal. Let us leave on our journey together, knowing that we can reach for the stars and together attain them."

One of many photo shoots: A gallop with Templado and Fasto through Gordes village in France, near where they live.

Templado's Early Stardom

Magali and I met in our early twenties when we were both working at the same riding school in Apt and we got married in 2003, on horseback of course—with many guests on horses too. Soon after we met we left to start our own riding school and we also devised a horse spectacular with which we toured France. Our participation at horse shows only reached a European dimension after that meeting with Pierre Lapouge in 1992 (described on p. 59) and appearing at the *Crinières d'Or* in Avignon. For the following two years we took part in a series of shows, with a friend, with acts consisting of an artistic mixture of trick riding, dressage, and liberty acts with Templado.

At the same time, Templado was in constant demand for television, advertisements, and commercials. In one ad for Tissot®, the watch company, the director wanted a stand-in for the child actor to gallop bareback across the sands pursued by twenty or so wild horses. My youngest brother, Mathieu, was already an experienced rider for a ten-year-old, and Templado knew him so I was not worried about him playing the part. It took only a couple of practice runs for Templado to understand exactly what he had to do. We tied an almost invisible cord round Templado's neck for Mathieu to hold onto. The camera rolled and off they went across the sands, pursued by wild Camargue horses that were being driven along by the extras. The commercial was a great success for Tissot.

For another shot the director asked if Templado could paw the ground with a scraping action. I bent down, spoke a word, and went through the motion myself. I only had to do it a couple of times and he grasped what was required; the camera rolled and Templado performed as if he had been doing it all his life. The director remarked that he wished he could find actors who picked things up so quickly.

Stallions Sharing the Spotlight

The chance encounter with Don Manuel Vidrié Gómez that took us to the Caribbean for two years had a great influence on the horses and on us. I had begun doing a regular act with Templado, but about this time I decided to expand the performance by working with two free stallions at the same time. I started preparing Amoroso, though Templado was furious at first. He was very jealous about me sharing my trust and affection with another horse. Amoroso was furthermore a rather aggressive horse so altogether it was a huge challenge. However, it began to work well so I decided to go a step further and add a third stallion to my liberty act: Aetes, a sensible character. Both new horses accepted Templado as the dominant one and the piece took shape. I have worked with up to six free stallions in front of an audience. Each horse requires a different level of energy to match his own and the concentration to achieve this can be exhausting.

CAVALIA

By the time our two-year contract in the Dominican Republic had expired, Magali and I knew that our horses had reached higher standards of technique that could possibly open other doors for us. We never stopped working on the horses' development but now was the time to add the other strands to our concept of shows: artistic attraction and entertainment. We were inspired by the *La Nouba* show in Orlando, Florida, and by *Arabian Nights* where we were employed by Mark Miller

Dao resting in his stall but all the while keeping a keen eye on any human or horse passing by. When the latter, Dao always made sure the horse knew who was boss.

as temporary trainers. An idea began to take shape: we wanted to combine the athletic and artistic achievements of our horses with a show that had original music, beautiful costumes, and spectacular trick riding.

During the next three years, we divided our time between taking part in European shows and working in the US principally at *Arabian Nights*. Meanwhile, our horses had extended holidays at home

Frédéric, Zenete, and Dao during a "tandem" act in their last show in France before going to Canada to begin Cavalia. After an incredible display of passage, piaffe, and galloping in tandem, Zenete was let loose and he performed cabrades and other movements at liberty. Much to Frédéric's surprise, he was given an award at this show by Les Haras Nationaux, a national organization that serves to protect the diversity of horse breeds existing in France.

in the south of France with Magali's parents whose farm was close by, so the horses led an idyllic life between engagements and were ready and happy to perform at the drop of a hat whenever we returned.

The opportunity to put into practice our idea of combining beauty and entertainment with high level dressage came as early as 1992 at Bezier, in France, when we were asked to participate in an important equestrian event. It was for us the first time that we were able to demonstrate our idea of a "horse spectacular." In a Roman setting with two tall broken pillars commanding the stage, and people in masks to give a touch of Venice for good measure, swirling smoke, musicians, and two dancers, we made up a show that combined all these elements with trick riding and a pas de deux, displaying the highest standards of dressage with two riders. The audience responded enthusiastically and we now knew our instincts were sound.

Normand Latourelle, a French Canadian and one of the original founders of Cirque du Soleil, wanted to do a show with horses in it, and had, by chance, seen a video of us at work. He realized that our ideas were very similar to his own. He met us, saw a show in Nimes and loved what we did. Investors came on board, and a show that celebrates the relationship between horses and humans, Cavalia, was born. A mixture of liberty acts, pas de deux, trick riding, human aerial acrobatics, live music, and wild costumes all fell into place. Many talented individuals helped make it happen, including choreographers, technical experts, creative artists, specialty horse trainers, and a cast of dancers, musicians, acrobats, and stunt riders.

Another bonus: Normand's wife, Dominique, did everything in her power to ensure the horses were given the best possible living conditions and was a constant support in any matter relating to their welfare. The importance of this can only be appreciated when you know that the number of horses expanded to more than sixty—all stallions and geldings—by the time the show opened.

Three performances had been planned for Shawinigan in Canada, and shortly before the first, the press was invited. The magnificent new tent, made in Italy, had only just gone up but none of the horses had been inside. Michel Cusson, who wrote the music for the show, was sitting on a chair playing the guitar. I came in with Templado and gave an impromptu performance; the cameras flashed, the videos rolled, and the next morning someone came to tell Magali that there was a line round the tent for tickets, selling about 300 an hour. Soon the 2,000 seats were sold out for all performances and we had to extend the run to fourteen shows.

Cavalia toured Canada and the United States and subsequently moved to Europe: to Belgium, Germany, Portugal, and Spain. After nearly six great years, two-million spectators, and 1,500 shows—seven performances a week and we never missed one, even when we had the occasional fever or flu—we left the show and were replaced by my younger brother, Mathieu, and Magali's sister, Estelle.

MY FAMILY BACKGROUND

My parents were raised in the same village and were the same age. They were friends from childhood. At only four years old they both fell in love with a little donkey that someone kept in a field in their village, Cavaillon, near Avignon, France. They started riding it regularly and went on expeditions into the countryside whenever they could persuade their parents to take them. They longed to have their own horses but their parents were against the idea so when my father and mother, both aged eighteen, secretly bought Arabian horses, they had to keep them at a friend's stable. Their parents could not hold out forever and when the young couple married they both arrived at the church on horseback, as did the guests.

Their passion for horses grew with the years and they began to take part in horse shows. They started their own stable and took in "problem" horses in order to help retrain them. They soon gained such a good reputation for being able to cope with and sort out difficult horses that people came from far and wide to seek their help. Unfortunately, the job became more and more frustrating and even dangerous because so many of the horses had been ill-treated and my father was quite seriously injured on his cheek while working with a particularly aggressive stallion. As a result, they finally decided to breed their own so they could raise horses properly from the time they were born.

During those years I had been given a wonderful opportunity to learn to handle every kind of difficult horse. The experience served me well. My father had a perfect instinct about the right moment to put a saddle on a young horse for the first time and when it was safe to mount. We never had a problem: when he gave me the go-ahead, I had complete confidence, and though I have ridden hundreds of young horses on our farm, often for the first time they were mounted, I have never fallen off. My father had not been formally taught how to ride and neither was I. It was all done by instinct and trial and error and by following his example.

Perdigon

By great good fortune a friend found my parents a five-year-old Spanish stallion from the Bororquez stud that perfectly conformed to the ideal they were looking for: a horse that combined beauty, grace of movement, good conformation, and temperament. He became the great Perdigon, the sire of our family stud and five years later, he was recognized by the Portuguese Lusitano Authority as one of the Spanish stallions "imported" to improve the Lusitano breed and could henceforth be known as one. He has had many fine sons and daughters and the line has undoubtedly been improved.

Our farm was in the middle of truly beautiful hilly countryside and my father was convinced that this had a beneficial effect on the horses: to smell the scents of flowers, trees, and grass; to become accustomed to a rabbit breaking cover in front of them or birds wheeling above them; and to gallop up and down hills was to reduce the level of stress in their life and give them wonderful muscle tone. He always says that this life in the country helps to relax them and keep their minds receptive to being trained.

My Mother's Part

My mother also made a big contribution to our breeding farm and to the horses' well-being. She was particularly interested in natural foods and would go to great lengths to search out what she decided was

Magali's father Pierrot on the great Perdigon at a village dressage show. At six years old, Perdigon already enjoyed the reputation of being the most handsome Spanish stallion in France. Thanks to Perdigon, Pierrot became well-known as a trainer and for his performances in horse spectaculars. Perdigon lived to be 37 and sired 200 foals.

Magali's parents, Pierrot and Joelle, were so devoted to their horses that Magali wonders how they could have had time for two daughters! But they did and it was—and is—a close family. They still put a mattress in the room next to the stall where a mare is giving birth. They had to sleep in some discomfort for a whole week waiting for Valiente, a son of Dao, born on April 25, 2009. Watch out for this one: he's already a star!

the right food for each horse. There were special mixes of carrots, artichokes, and seaweed with different grains—most of the products that can be bought these days as manufactured supplements—and trays of germinating seeds that were fed to the animals. I remember pounds of cherry stalks being infused to produce a diuretic. She was also ahead of her time in the use of homeopathic remedies like arnica. My grandmother had enjoyed a reputation as a healer of horses and had passed on to her daughter a deep understanding of the uses of different wild plants—both for humans and for horses—either to improve health or heal illness. I have inherited some of this ability and have good instincts about wild herbs and mushrooms—we eat a lot of them and are still alive to tell the tale!

My Upbringing

My upbringing was so naturally combined with the life and care of our horses that I cannot imagine what a life without horses would be like.

I and my sister Estelle, who is six years younger, had always to think of the horses' welfare first thing on getting up and last thing before bedtime. I think of my childhood as being, from my earliest memories, involved with horses and lived at their rhythm.

Magali at home on her first quadruped. Already, she has good leg position but she's not paying attention to where she is going!

And on Chiquito with her grandfather "Pepe" Delgado keeping a watchful eye while chewing a stick of "reglisse" (licorice).

We rode to school on ponies (mine was named Chiquito), which we shared with our less fortunate classmates. It was a very special school with an unusual approach to education: in the morning we studied in our classroom but in the afternoon, the teachers took us on expeditions in the surrounding countryside and into the hills where we were taught about the wonders of nature; learned to respect every living creature; and came to understand the passage of the seasons, the growing of crops, and rearing of livestock. I was so concerned about all animals, both large and small, that I persuaded my schoolmates to treat every animal with the same respect that I did. I must have been a holy terror, as I would not allow any cruelty, even the killing of an insect!

Quite early in my childhood my parents began to attend equestrian events or "spectaculars" and it was not long before I would accompany them, at first alone and later with my little sister. Soon we were producing our own little acts, along with our parents—Mother did a lasso act and Father did trick riding and dressage.

By the time I was eighteen, my parents were participating in horse spectaculars with more than a dozen horses and had begun their own breeding operation. They were enterprising people and were the first in our part of the world to travel in horse shows in other European countries such as Belgium and Spain. We went great distances and, at night, bedded down with the horses not only for their security but to save ourselves the expense of lodgings. As a result, we built up our understanding and trust in each other and all in the most natural and unforced way.

FRÉDÉRIC'S GIFT

Frédéric was the first person I met whose views were so similar to my own that we hardly needed to discuss an approach to dealing with any horse. Right from the start, there were so many areas where we agreed that we could address the nub of a problem very quickly. I might add that I am also his number one fan when it comes to his paintings and drawings. As for music, we usually had the same likes and dislikes.

Although I had always been brought up to treat horses with respect and kindness, Frédéric gave me the shared conviction that work can have better results if it is channeled through game-playing where the notion of pleasure and freedom to show initiative and invention are paramount. Our shared experience in the taming of Templado taught me, as it did Fred, that in many ways one has to allow the usual roles to be reversed: what can I do for the horse and not just, what can the horse do for me?

DAO

A key moment in our lives was my second place at Grand Prix level in 2002 in Rouen, France, in the annual national dressage competition where I beat the French Champion. I believe that I am the first rider from an equestrian spectacular background to have competed successfully at the top level of international dressage. The dressage world has a slightly exclusive air to it and I think some of the riders looked a bit askance at someone like me daring to enter and compete with true professionals on their terms. However, they soon accepted that my methods were different; they were intrigued and gave me no real problems.

What excited me was the ability and opportunity to make the crossover between two distinct parts of the horse world and, in particular, ones that had enjoyed little or no contact. The top dressage world tended to look down on the equine spectacular as little more than circus acts, and these performers, in turn, were not much concerned with Grand Prix level dressage riding—though, of course, many of them had reached a high standard of equitation. I was determined to connect the two worlds to prove to people that neither was exclusive. I wanted to bring the idea of pleasure and enjoyment to dressage competition and the high standards of dressage competition to the world of horse spectaculars.

Magali on Dao prepare for a half-pass to the left and then perform an extended trot. These were taken early on in Dao's dressage career, but he was already beginning to win competitions. He impressed judges with his natural ability. For a Lusitano, he did a good extended trot, but at piaffe and passage, he was exceptional—often scoring "9s."

Nearly all the horses used at the top dressage levels are Warmbloods, many of them breeds from Germany, Holland, and Denmark, ideally suited to the movements required: in competition, the horse has to demonstrate, in addition to all the basic gaits, pirouettes at the canter, flying changes, piaffe, and passage. The conformation of these horses is ideal for higher level dressage tests—to give an example, in the walk and trot, one can commonly see scores of "9" out of a possible "10." And I enter with Dao, my beautiful Lusitano, a horse breed seldom seen at this level of competition and not as well suited to scoring high in the walk and trot. (Lusitanos typically score much lower—say a "5"—though I have managed to squeeze Dao up a point or two.) However, he is superb at the other movements, and at the Grand Prix in Rouen he did me proud. In piaffe and passage he scored "8s" without effort.

It had only taken five attempts at Grand Prix level for Dao to attain this second place. His first entry had gained him a fourteenth out of twenty-four competitors. The next year he was eighth, then sixth, fifth, and finally second. He rather disliked Grand Prix at first because

Dao winning second place in competition with all the best dressage riders in France: Serge Cornu, Dominique d'Esmé, Marietta Almasy, and Odile van Doorn—the winner—who is on Magali's left and who became French champion at the end of the year. It was a huge honor for Magali to place in this company.

he adores music and applause, and in those days, Grand Prix tests were considered too serious for levity of this sort. Now, of course, there is a Grand Prix test ridden to music known as the "Freestyle" or "Kur."

Because of his result in this competition, Dao was chosen along with seven other top-ranked horses for Bernard Morel, the international judge, to consider for the special honor and rank of "Dressage Horse." Only one or two are usually given this "label": Dao was one of the few that year and even his sons now bear the honorary title thanks to this achievement. It is a recognition of quality that is considered to have improved the Lusitano breed.

Frédéric Demonstrates Work at Liberty

After the competition the organizer, who knew about our "other" sort of performances, asked if, at the evening affair, Frédéric would give a demonstration. Fred explained that the horses he performed his liberty acts with were at home; there was only Dao who had just completed this strenuous dressage test. The organizer persisted and Fred was still hesitating when one of the competitors, who had heard about the possibility of such a performance, remarked disparagingly that it was not the time or place for a "circus act."

The gauntlet was thus thrown down and Fred took it up! From my point of view it was a heaven-sent opportunity to reinforce my own achievement in the Grand Prix and to demonstrate to the dressage world what we could offer them. Later, while the other dressage horses enjoyed their well-earned rest, Fred walked back to the arena leading Dao by a simple neck strap.

Frédéric tells the story of what happened next: "When I entered and released Dao, he took off like greased lightning. I'm sure a lot of the spectators thought it would be the last I would see of him! When he'd had a bit of a gallop he turned and came toward me; I could see that he was already responding to the audience made up of judges and competitors as well as spectators, rising to the occasion and beginning to lift his legs elegantly. It was no problem for me to run alongside, give the right signals, and see Dao soon doing a superb Spanish walk—rather unusually, he does this movement as well without a rider as he does with one.

"We went through some movements, performing cabrades and piaffe. Dao also sat, knelt, and lay down on the ground, which was easy to get him to do because he loves lying down, and I just had to watch for the smallest giveaway sign and then continue the movement with my own body. A clap of my hands and a quick word: Dao was up and galloping again. He ended in the 'reverence' position facing the audience, dropping gracefully down on one front knee and extending the other leg straight out ahead, with his head down and aligned with his back. They rose to their feet as one and gave us a standing ovation.

"Afterward, Magali spoke to the judges who said how wonderful it was to see a horse like Dao, happy and relaxed and not showing any signs of the stress displayed by so many horses that are brought to the Grand Prix level of dressage. But what we were most proud of was that we had shown these people in the sophisticated world of competitive dressage a horse performing the same steps that high level horses with top class riders achieve, but at liberty, without stress and with an evident sense of enjoyment.

"After the performance, I turned Dao out into a small paddock, something we always do when there is one available. A trainer came up to me. 'You mustn't do that,' he said. 'This horse is far too valuable to be left unguarded in a paddock.' I was shocked that someone would consider I might deprive a horse of his usual reward because he had done well and gained in value."

Dao lets his hair down and has a good roll at the end of a competition. Back to being a normal horse!

Reading Dao's Thoughts

Dao became for me what Templado was for Frédéric. I took him on as a two-year-old when he had given no sign of his quality. He was rather gawky and his head looked a bit out of proportion to his body but quite soon after his second birthday, he blossomed. He became all that I could ask for in a horse. He has a great ability to concentrate his energy but at the same time, he remains calm. He understands and learns quickly, he is noble and generous, he likes to do things properly, he is very rarely naughty and has the ability to tell me when I ask too much of him. He knows how to set limits and because of this I understand and respect his wishes. He is always charming with me. I remember once when I was being interviewed and filmed with him, the director asked me what he was thinking at that moment. I took one look at him and could see that he was very bored and wanted to get back to his stall. I began to explain this but before I had finished Dao took off at a gallop and went "home."

Dao expresses himself in his movement and in his deportment. He is concentrated, energetic, tries to understand, and assimilates quickly. Of course, like any horse, Dao has his ups and downs: if I am working with him and see from his demeanor that he is a little upset, I

Magali takes a moment to "read Dao's thoughts" after a bareback gallop along the shore at Paradise Cove, Malibu, California.

always stop the work and spend some time letting him play a favorite game or just simply being with him. I do not leave him if he has not recovered his spirits. Dao is always happy to repeat something until he is confident that he can do it. On the other hand, he shows discontent when I go too far: if I ask too much of him he pays no attention, he simply ignores me.

Dao's Sense of Fun

Here's another little story that demonstrates his certain quirky sense of fun. During a television filming session, he was to be filmed going across the set from one side to the other. We had practiced it a number of times and I was not expecting any problem but when the camera began to roll, Dao, instead of going in a straight line, trotted round the back of the director's desk and—I think accidentally, since he likes dogs—stepped on the director's basset hound. I don't know why he did this but when he makes up his mind to do something he does it!

He has sired several marvelous sons and they all seem to have inherited this rather amusing and quirky side to his nature. The other day I was watching one of them, Talento, as he sniffed a "flower" that turned out to be a thistle. It pricked him so he started "grubbing it up" with his hoof. At that moment his mother called from the other side of the field but he wouldn't obey her summons until he had completely finished off the offending plant: absolutely single-minded like his father.

Championship of France

In 1994, I entered Dao into the Young Horse Championships of France and he came second in his category of three year olds—a great surprise to those who had seen him only a year before. When four years old, he came first, with our horse Bandolero taking second place, but Dao went on to be Champion of the Lusitano winners in all categories, a feat he repeated at seven years old. I was then offered €200,000 (about $280,000) for him by Portuguese breeders but, of course, I turned the offer down. How could I have done otherwise, even though this would have been to us an enormous sum of money and one that would have

Waiting for the presentation of Breed Champion of the Year, in Avignon, France. Notice the "scarf" around Dao's neck— he had already won the Lusitano Breed Championship. This award was for the "Champion of Champions."

Magali performing at Equitana on Dao without bridle and saddle. It was a big step in their relationship when Dao showed sufficient trust to dance like this in front of an audience. It was only a year before when Magali first risked a gallop in the countryside without a bridle. Magali has known Dao since he was born.

enabled us to set up our stable the way we wanted it to be. The horse that had won the year before Dao was sold to breeders and was dead by the age of ten, worn out and finished. I could not have done that to Dao and lived with the knowledge, for any price.

Dao has not only gone on to be everything I have asked of him but is till going strong at nineteen.

Riding without Saddle or Bridle

One day, inspired no doubt by Fred's liberty work, I decided to risk going out for a hack on Dao with nothing but a neck strap. Don't forget, this was a powerful stallion. At first, I went a short way along the road toward the big field where we gallop but then I turned back, even though he

He is the only horse in whom she has such complete trust and confidence in any situation—she can say she has total trust in him. She knows he would never let her down. In these photos you can see his "soft" eyes—he is ignoring the 7,000 spectators, the lights, the applause. He is concentrating on her and in a state of perfect ease and comfort.

showed no signs of misbehaving. The next day, I went further and it was fine, so on the following day I went all the way to the field. I remember reaching it and breaking into a gallop. It was as if Dao recognized that I had put my trust in him and we galloped and galloped and galloped.

I felt the sort of pure joy that one can only hope to experience once or twice in a lifetime. I was quite overcome and at one point released the neckband, threw up my arms, let out a shout that would have pleased my Spanish ancestors and that Frédéric heard as he watched nervously from our home. I knew that Dao was feeling the same emotions. I shall never forget that moment and nor will Frédéric who, even though he was so far away, could understand exactly what was taking place and says it is one of the best memories in his life. From then on, I have regularly performed haute école dressage numbers in our productions with just a neckband and without a saddle.

On the first occasion that I made an appearance without saddle or bridle—at a performance in Paris with thousands of spectators—I suddenly had the feeling that Dao was going to do something naughty, which was unusual. Frédéric was waiting near the exit in case Dao panicked when he saw an enormous enlarged picture of himself and me on the gigantic screen above us. He had obviously become aware of it; I spoke to him and turned his head away. He recovered and did a faultless series of piaffe, passage, jambette, tempi changes, and pirouettes, finally lying down so that I could step calmly off. It was superb.

A favorite act in *Cavalia* that Fred and I did together, started with Fred walking into the arena. I came in mounted on Gracioso, saddled and bridled, walked up to Fred and did a sequence of piaffe, pirouette, passage, Spanish walk, and jambette, all very precisely in time with the music. Suddenly, Dao appeared without saddle or bridle and galloped around the arena a few times before coming up to me. I dismounted and Fred helped me up onto Dao's back. Then I performed all the same dressage moves, to the same standard, with only a simple neckband.

"Dao, we've got to win."

With Dao, I took first prize in the Kur Baroque dressage competition at Equitana in Essen, Germany. We won this competition (held every two years for all horses other than German horses) twice running, so Dao was Champion for four years. It is one of the biggest equestrian events in Europe. On the second occasion, I knew it would be the last time that I could ask Dao to compete at this level. We were off to America shortly and by the time we got back he would be too old; this event would be the end of his competitive career in Europe. I remember the day: at the same time as the competition took place we were giving performances at the *Hot Top* musical show in the city. Fred and I performed three of the twenty acts for ten days running so I knew that many of the spectators watching the dressage competition would have seen me performing in our show and be "on my side." But that only heightened the tension as I watched the other competitors go on and perform. Then our moment arrived. I said to Dao, "Dao, we've got to win." Never had I felt a closer union with him.

Dao at the biennial Kur Baroque at Equitana in Essen, Germany. Dao won this event twice running and was therefore champion for four years. The second time was unforgettable when the German audience—always a perceptive one— clapped in rhythm to the music during the Kur. Many of the people watching had seen Magali perform the same dressage movements—without saddle and bridle—in the horse show spectacular that was on at the same time every evening in town, and were happy to show their appreciation of her and Dao's dual skills. Neither Frédéric nor Magali have yet come across another horse who combines the qualities necessary for competitive dressage work at the highest level with the communication and artistic abilities needed to shine in the horse spectacular world.

We entered and halted, I made the salute, the music began, and we went straight into a piaffe. At that instant I knew we were going to win. Dao was faultless in everything. The audience of several thousand began to applaud. The sound rose to a crescendo as though they knew the outcome. Dao was in perfect balance and in perfect rhythm with the music that Fred had arranged for us. In the wings, Fred and my sister Estelle watched me enter and later they told me that at that same moment they too looked at each other and said, "They're going to win." When it was over, the judge remarked on the loud speaker that it was wonderful to see such an artistic display—for which I was given a "9"—and that he wished there were more performances like it.

I had achieved one of my greatest ambitions, which as I've already mentioned, is to demonstrate that there is no impenetrable divide between the horse spectacular performance world designed to bring pleasure to audiences in a theater, and the dressage world, designed to encourage technical excellence and beauty of movement with competition in mind. Previously this wish had seemed almost impossible to achieve. For example, there was an occasion earlier in Paris when I rode a dressage test at midday and was going to perform in the evening at a spectacular. The judges heard about this and were so displeased that they deliberately marked me down. However, the audience at the competition, and later the press, were in no doubt about what had happened and were outraged by the judges' bias.

Quelam, an Impertinent Youngster

Only time will tell if we can ever produce another great champion like Dao. Another Templado would also seem impossible because he "broke the mold" of an age, he was a one-off. But with our approach to training, it is at least theoretically possible that we could reach the summit again. It would hardly be fair to other trainers: we have had two extraordinary horses and many top trainers wait all their life for just one.

However Quelam, one of Dao's sons, is coming along well. So far, I can say with confidence that he has never experienced conflict; he doesn't know how to say, "No!" because I have only asked easy things of him. He has reached that magical age of about three years old when coltish looks are cast away and the young horse expands into his adult form. Until that moment, one never quite knows how a horse will turn out but already Quelam is warning us of his "kingly" status. The older generation in the stable exchange knowing looks as if they know they will have to give way to this impertinent youngster who walks proudly past their stalls.

Magali and Quelam at two and then at three years old, beginning to work and the first time he had a saddle on his back. In-hand work continues as if there isn't a saddle to make him forget about it. Here he is doing a little jambette. And at four, mounted for the first time. Magali asks nothing except for him to accept her weight and the fact that she is "higher" than him instead of being at his side. This is the result of months of preparation. Quelam is a son of Dao and a mare belonging to the French actress Veronique Jeannot. He loves play, shows a lot of expression, and is generally very promising. So far, Magali has been able to avoid any negative behavior with him: she has never had to chide or really say "No" to him.

Templado and Dao

I have been peculiarly blessed with Dao. It was extraordinary enough for us to have Templado but with him we learned the lessons that helped us turn Dao into a dressage star of his time. It is interesting to compare these two exceptional horses: when they passed near each other, as with two Greek Gods, lightning flashed and thunder rolled. Understandably, there was little love lost between them and we could never put them in box stalls next to each other. They were both masters of all they surveyed and the way in which they achieved domination was very different. When he entered the stable, Templado trumpeted his rank and the other horses came to the front of their stall and stared

Dao and Magali on the beach in Malibu, California. These are the sorts of tender, privileged moments that reinforce their relationship for every activity, even Grand Prix competition. All Magali's work and experience is rewarded by moments like these!

at him before they bowed their head and went on with their food. When Dao enters the stable, he makes not a sound but draws himself up like an actor coming on stage. The other horses recognize his gait and again they come to the front of their stall; one can see from the way they look at him that they recognize his superiority as a leader.

If we are right that our approach to raising and training horses allows them to realize their full potential, then, with the horses emerging from my parents' stud, we might expect to produce some more champions in the future. I am constantly on the lookout for a horse like Dao who might go right to the top of the dressage competition world. It will require skill, patience, and of course, luck. You don't find a champion under every stone!

Our Practical Approach 5

The first thing is to decide what indeed are your aims with a horse; it is the same for Magali and me as it is for you. Is it a horse to ride out in the countryside that you want? Is the horse for jumping, or dressage, or a Western sport like reining? Different activities bring different demands and responsibilities. In my case, I want to be able to use my horses "on stage" in four or five shows a week. This is a fairly extreme goal and I have to constantly be on the lookout to see if I am overdoing things. If I think I might be, I need to have the necessary courage to stop and say, "The horses' welfare comes first."

I also want to be able to go out alone with a horse and enjoy his company. This is another kind of goal altogether and probably closer to that of many who read this book. It shows that you can have more than one, but I think it is important to be aware of your aims so that you can monitor them and their effects on the horse. I am always conscious that my first responsibility to the horses is to see that they are happy and enjoy doing what they do. I ask my horses to give a tremendous amount and I work very hard in return. I spend my days with my horses; I give my life to them and it would be impossible to be happily married if Magali and I were not both doing the same thing.

Assume that I am making a start with a new horse, one that I have not seen or worked with before. Firstly, I always strive to keep my principles in mind however difficult the horse might sometimes be. I

have to remind myself that as I begin to gain the trust and respect of the horse, so the difficulties will ease. Faced with a new horse that has only known the wrong sort of treatment, I have to be endlessly patient.

LEARN TO "READ" YOUR HORSE

I take into account a horse's mental and physical traits before I decide on my approach to the exercises and the playing we will do together. In case it is not already clear, what I mean by "playing" is that I create a relaxed atmosphere of enjoyment and fun. Each horse may need a slightly different approach to achieve this state, which is essential to success, but the principles are the same.

The horse makes signals with every part of his body. I have to learn to read his thoughts by watching his nostrils, his ears, his eyes,

After a photo session, Frédéric and Magali let off steam with Dao and Fasto in their meadow at home. Fasto does a cabrade as an "explosion" of joy and fun.

and his general attitude. His eyes are particularly important to learn to read because they are like an opening through which I can see what is going on inside his head. He is telling me with subtle signals how he feels. Is he happy? Once we start working or playing, I ask myself, is he satisfied with what we have done together? I try to remember at what moment I was aware of progress and how I achieved it.

Misunderstanding produces an even greater barrier between us than ill treatment. Understanding will, on the other hand, begin to forge a link between the two of us. I will begin to feel that I am on the same wavelength as my horse and that he is accepting me.

Well, you have to get to know the horse, and you will make more progress if you do not start by immediately asking him to do something. My own technique is to set him loose—in an enclosed area, of course—and to watch him. I let him express his feelings without any constraint and I soon begin to form an idea of his nature. A state of

Templado was an expert at "reading" people. Frédéric could always learn something by introducing a person to Templado and then watching his reaction. It was often remarked that Templado gave you the impression he was looking through you. Bandolero, known as a cremello—note his pink skin and blue eyes—has delicate eyes and finds it difficult to see in the shade. This photo shows his soft, confident eye. Guizo's eyes change radically with every change of mood so he is usually quite easy to read. Here he seems relaxed and interested.

Lyrico looks at himself in the mirror in the arena. This is an interesting moment as Lyrico sees his own image. At first, he thinks it's another horse with a pleasant expression because he has one. An aggressive horse will see another horse looking at him aggressively and often attack the mirror. In this case, Lyrico went behind the mirror to check, accepted that it was not another horse, lost interest, and wandered off.

liberty also allows me to introduce myself to him in the politest possible way. I watch how he reacts to my approaching him and coming a little closer. I begin to read him: Is he cool or stressed? What sounds does he make? How does he react to the movements of my body? How does he react to being touched or simply to being looked at? What effect does the sound of my voice have? If I am holding a whip or a crop, is he aware of it, and does he react if I move it?

Is there tension in his face? Are his nostrils dilated or relaxed? What is the expression in his eyes—are they alert, or bored, or resigned, or fearful? How is his body moving? Are his shoulders and hindquarters working together or is there more energy at one end of the body than the other? Is he collected and coordinated or loose and sloppy? Is he easily distracted by what he sees going on around him?

Is he shaking his head, and if so, what does this suggest? What is he doing with his tail? Is he placing his feet evenly or is he favoring one of them? How does he hold his head or his neck? Is there a weakness in his body that needs attention—such as evidence of a weak back? When I am close to him, how does he smell? Horses, like people, can smell differently in varying states of health, and a sour unpleasant odor, especially down the side of a horse's face, can be an indication of stress or poor health.

Observations in the Stall

Even at rest, you can learn much from observing your horse. Take the ears for example: what might his ear movements mean? If a horse moves his weight from foot to foot, does this indicate something? And what about when he shakes his withers? How do you interpret the look of his eye? Is it a "soft" or a "hard" eye, and what does this mean about him? How does your horse stand in his stall when he is contented? If he is unhappy, does he stand differently? If he has an uncomfortable feeling in his stomach does he not show this by the way he stands?

It would be so convenient if I could give you hard and fast answers to all these questions, but life is not so simple. You could not do such a thing in the analysis of human behavior. What I *can* say to you is watch out for *all* these indications; allow your instincts to tell you what your senses observe. Very soon you will automatically take in the things you have

Nacarado at four years old. He is very demanding of attention and curious about everything. A lovely character and notice his terrific movement. You can always learn more by observing a horse when he is expressing himself, like this. Magali works on contact with Nacarado, and tries to understand his particular needs. You can see him looking for reassurance from her. Frédéric and Magali hope Nacarado is a future star.

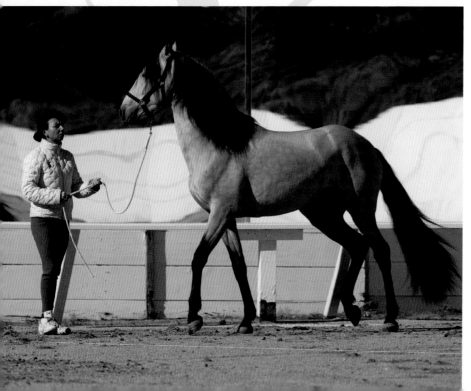

learned to look for and you will have the ability to look for other more subtle signs. You will also see that the same signal does not have the same root cause for every horse or even for the same horse every day.

At this point, you may throw up your hands and say that this is all too ambiguous and too much to learn. But you have already learned to do all these things with other people. When you meet with someone you know well after you have been apart for a time, can't you see in an instant when something is wrong? Why should "reading" a horse not be similar?

The Importance of Concentration

I always watch the horse with every fiber of my being: I not only try to read him with my senses of sight, hearing, and smell, I concentrate my mind on communicating my own thoughts and listening to his. I concentrate so hard that other thoughts are excluded.

People understand that there are situations in everyday life demanding total concentration; mysteriously, it may not occur to the same people that, in dealing with a horse, there is the same requirement. Perhaps someone will allow himself and the horse to be interrupted by a phone call, which not only breaks the person's own concentration, but that of the horse. When you work with a horse you ask him to leave whatever he is doing and pay attention to you. You are trying to reach the same wavelength as that of the horse and, if you allow an interruption on your end, you are being disrespectful to him. We humans may be able to switch on and off, or from one subject to another, at the drop of a hat but a horse is not so flexible. If he has decided to give you the benefit of his full concentration, and you lightly drop it because something more important to you crops up, he might not want to risk giving you the same degree of attention again.

I often use breathing to relax both the horse and myself, and to help develop concentration. I breathe out in a way the horse can understand and copy. All my horses learn to do this even if, like Guizo, it takes a long time. With him it took me a whole year but as soon as he understood and began to breathe with me he became much more relaxed. When I am doing this work, I like to be alone and not have other people present or watching me.

Guizo was, at first, a rather tense and complex horse. He needed a lot of time spent on him to build his confidence. Learning to breathe calmly has helped to break the barrier.

LET YOUR IDEA BECOME THE HORSE'S IDEA!

Gracil is a wonderful horse but not always easy. He puts up mental barriers, and I have to find a way round them or get rid of them. I have to focus all my energy on the problem. If, for example, he refuses to back out of the horse trailer the usual way and will not respond to being pulled, then I might turn him around and push him. "Ah!" he then thinks, "That was my idea!" To make your idea the same as the horse's is the best possible solution to many problems. (Read more about Gracil on the next page.)

USE OF THE WHIP

Some horses never lose their fear of whips and we should avoid risking this happening. In general, horse trainers use the whip in such a way that the horse interprets it as an aggressive instrument. The whip has to become a passive aid: one that the horse does not fear and accepts as there to help him understand or to initiate or stimulate a movement. A whip can be used in a positive way for a large spectrum of actions. I often use it to touch and to guide by producing the feeling that life would be better for the horse if it were not there. Or, it can be used as a form of authority like a stop signal. However, it must not be viewed by the horse as something always to be feared and avoided. It is tempting to think of the whip as an instrument of aggression, but in fact, it is only the person holding it who can be aggressive.

When working with a horse at liberty, I often use a whip or stick, but only as a guide. I might rest it gently on the horse's flank but my aim is to be able to hold it about a foot away from the horse when he understands its function. I may use my voice to stop a horse doing something wrong, then raise my voice and finally tap the horse on the chest, but not so as to hurt him and only when I am certain that the horse will think that my use of the whip or stick is justified.

ATTRACTING AND HOLDING ATTENTION

There are many ways of attracting a horse's attention and there is no reason why you should not discover new ones. I often run, either toward or away from the horse. In an arena with wooden sides or fencing, or in the stage enclosure where we perform our shows, I may tap on a board with my crop. I may walk slowly about or keep still. I may use my voice.

Each "language" has different "words" that are effective. Whatever method I use, the essential thing is not to cause opposition. If one doesn't work I try another, and as soon as I capture the horse's attention I congratulate him. Closely allied to this I try always to avoid failure: I never set the horse an impossible task—impossible, that is, in relation to his fears. Avoid a "check," let alone a "checkmate" situation at all costs. Gracil, for example, is fearful of wooden platforms, so I never ask him to mount one before I have climbed onto it myself to give him confidence. Then he is fine. The same applies to ramps into vans and horse trailers—though in this case, as I relate in chapter 6, he enters a van easily but needs reassurance before leaving.

There are those who recommend not looking the horse in the eye, or even speaking to him or touching him in case he interprets this as an act of aggression. Magali and I both find that we can—and do—look the horse in the eye, as well as using both touch and speech. I find I give the horse confidence by using *all* my senses. It is my belief that many horses look on us humans without preformed ideas—such as that we are necessarily aggressors—so it is vitally important to maintain this state of mind.

As for holding the horse's attention, part of the secret is not to make the exercises too long—especially when an exercise is new. We never work on a new exercise until the horse becomes bored, which can happen in as little as 15 minutes. As soon as we see signs of boredom, we change to some other activity, and it is best to do this *before* you see the signs! A typical pattern for us would be: play, reward with a caress, cabrade, relax, caress, Spanish walk, caress, and so forth. When improving an exercise the horse already knows, you can work for a longer time, which has the added advantage of building up the right muscles for that exercise and making it easier for the horse.

LIBERTY WORK CHALLENGES VERSUS MOUNTED WORK

In work at liberty, problems occur that might not be evident when mounted. Though one may not be aware of them when riding, they are still present, so knowing about them and having to cope with them during liberty work increases your ability to deal with them under saddle. The main difficulty in transferring what you can tell of the horse at liberty to your mounted practice is that when the horse is free, you communicate with each other through body language, as well, of course, as the mind. When riding, communication is principally through the seat, the hands, and the balance of the rider—and, again, the mind.

Whether it is liberty work or mounted, the essential element for both is that there should be no tension. Tension is a negative quality. When there is tension during an exercise, repetition only repeats the negative quality, which is then reinforced. The other day I was teaching Delirio to put his front foot on a box for the first time. I took his foot in my hand and gently placed it on the box. Then I stepped back and watched him absorb this new experience. He seemed relaxed about it, but I was not absolutely certain, so I did something else as a diversion before returning to the new exercise. When I came back to it, I was in no doubt that he accepted it without any tension or anxiety.

The natural reaction of a horse to something he does not know is very often opposition. If there is opposition then it is essential to avoid conflict by going round the problem in some way.

EXCHANGING ENERGIES

Horses fluctuate enormously in the amount of energy they put out. This is not so noticeable to a mounted rider but imagine yourself on foot with loose stallions in a performance. They may appear to be acting in perfect unison but what is happening to achieve this? The answer is that there is an enormous variation in the amount of energy being put out by the trainer and, when there is more than one horse, different levels of energy directed at each one. The only way to deal with a horse's energy when you are on foot is with your own energy, at the appropriate level to control that of the horse—and of each horse when there is more than one. I must be able to expand and contract the amount of energy that I put out. I am told by people watching me that the variation is often clearly visible: I seem to grow taller and broader when I am increasing the level. Conversely I shrink when I need to put out less.

Not only do I shrink or expand but also my gaze is more or less intense, my voice sharper or gentler, and the movements of my whip more or less authoritative. My breathing is exaggerated so that the horse is conscious of whether I am exhaling or inhaling. I remember watching Linda Tellington-Jones at work and it was clear that the use of her diaphragm was an essential part of the control of her energy. I have the impression that my strength emanates from somewhere around my diaphragm; it is definitely involved with the breath.

When I "turn on the power" I have to be careful not to do so for too long or I may damage my relationship with the horse. It was like that with Phoebus one day when he turned away from me during a show. I had to sweeten my voice and lower my energy for him to return and carry on with the performance.

Magali says, "When mounted one has to think as much about receiving messages as of giving them out. An example might be the occasion when I got the message from Dao that we were going to win the biennial Kur championship at *Equitana*. He showed me that his breathing was relaxed and in time with mine. This in turn greatly increased my confidence and calmness.

"If I want to do a Spanish walk, or any movement that requires a lot of energy, and I think the horse's energy level is too low, I have first to reinforce his energy. I raise my own energy in order to share

Templado, Fasto, and Aetes perform at Equitana in Essen, Germany. All stallions require different levels of energy to control them. Frédéric has to read them very quickly and adjust the energy he is putting out for each horse. Here you see Fasto, in the middle, wandering out a bit and Templado helping to push him back into the right position. Frédéric is saluting the public, therefore losing a little control, which accounts for Fasto's wandering. Then, a large circle to the left, probably following some cabrades, so the stallions are all full of energy and a bit difficult to control. Aetes is "connected" but Fasto is not. However, Frédéric knows that Templado will bring him back into the circle. Frédéric talks to Fasto to calm him down and recapture his attention as they all slow to a walk. Templado served as the "guide" for the other stallions. It was only when Templado was no longer performing that Frédéric really appreciated how much he owed the stallion. It is now more difficult for him to work with three horses at liberty, because he has never found another horse that filled this "helping" role in quite the same way.

it with him so that we both have the same level. You can change the energy level of your horse—and sometimes it has to be lessened rather than increased. For example, Bandolero has an unusually high energy level and is often so energetic that I have to work hard to calm him down and reduce it."

Concentrate with Mind and Body

"Whether I am putting out more or less energy I am always concentrated on what I am doing," Magali continues. "I am telling the horse with my mind and my body and, as Fred has already said, the horse can immediately detect if my mind is elsewhere. Whether it is that they interpret this dichotomy as a lack of respect or whether because of their sense of independence—or possibly even their sense of fun— you may suddenly find yourself losing control. If you are out for a trail ride you might get away with a lack of concentration but if you are performing advanced dressage steps you will not, and do not blame the horse if he does something unscripted that you consider wrong. It is your fault if your mind was elsewhere at the time.

"In her book *What Horses Say*, Julie Dicker tells a story about a woman who was having problems with her horse who suddenly started shying and generally misbehaving. The vet could find nothing wrong so he asked Julie who spoke to the horse and learned that his owner used to ride him alone but now went out with a friend and spent the whole time chatting with her. The horse was trying to tell his owner that he was not happy with this change of practice. The owner was amazed and admitted this was the case so she stopped 'chatting' and the bad behavior cleared.

"If I am in a show and I see my horse looking around him and not fully concentrating, I first bring him to order with all the mental and physical cues at my disposal. When he has started concentrating again I relax the signals that I have been using to bring him to that state. I'm sure that there are manuals on horsemanship that tell you to tap the horse on the nose when he tries to bite you—but if you do not concentrate your energy on what you are doing at the same time, you will be less successful in achieving your end. Your intention must be clear to the horse."

FIRST IMPRESSIONS ARE OFTEN RIGHT

You can be wrong but often the first impression is the right one. People often ask me, "How do you know that the horse is suffering or that he's anxious?" It is not easy for me to reply to this because my understanding has become largely instinctive. I say to apprentice trainers, "Try to *feel* what the horse is saying to you." Remember, you can usually work out what people around you are thinking without having recourse to the spoken word. Are they relaxed? Are they unhappy? You can do the same with horses once you apply yourself to the task. Why is that horse moving away from you? Is he nervous or does he want to play? These two alternatives will produce different telltale signs and you must pick them up. Perhaps you decide that he wants to play so you start a game. How does he respond? If you were right, remember the signs that made you take that decision. I also use my voice a lot. I speak to the horse and watch his reactions. Some horses are very attentive to my voice, which they often betray by turning their ears toward me. Other horses show no such reaction.

TOUCHING, SCRATCHING, AND A "CUDDLE"

I touch horses more or less all over with the palm of my hand. I also use a scratching motion, sometimes light as a feather and at other times, a really deep action. I watch closely to see how they react to this contact. What areas disturb them and what areas reassure them?

I think about what I have sensed and try to fit the information into a pattern for this particular horse. Each one, needless to say, may be quite different, and you have to remember which areas bring pleasure or disturb. A horse will soon show you where he wants to be touched or scratched and for how long, by positioning his body alongside you in such a way that you can easily reach the indicated part. When he has had enough he simply moves away.

This was so true of Templado and indeed all the sons of Perdigon. After Templado had stopped performing but still traveled with us, however tiring the show was and however late the hour, I would go to see him and spend some time with him at the end of the day. He showed me immediately where he wanted me to massage him to within a few centimeters, and when he'd had enough he simply moved to another position. (We find that all the sons of Perdigon like being scratched on the neck and sons of Zagalote on the croup!)

If Lancelot arrives on the stage and I see that he's tense, I scratch him on the withers. When I do this he extends his neck and makes a face, which gets a laugh from the audience. Some nights I go to scratch him and he moves a pace forward or backward, or even paws the ground when he's had enough as if to say that he's okay. Occasionally I can see that he's not okay, and I'm not quite sure why he has this reaction. I'm still hoping to understand him! (I tell you a little more about Lancelot on p. 135.)

Sometimes a horse just needs "a cuddle," but it is essential to establish rules of contact before giving way. If he respects the rules then a cuddle can give exactly the reassurance he needs. Lancelot often asks for one, whereas Templado rarely did so.

When I have a problem with my back I go to my osteopath and he tells me he is "listening through his hands" to what is going on. I try doing the same with my horses.

In a sense the ultimate physical contact is when you ride the horse, particularly bareback. People ask me if horses really enjoy being ridden. Provided you have gained their confidence and respect before you mount, I think the answer is, yes. The bodily contact with you can make your horse feel good and deepen your special relationship with him—with all the expected provisos. Possibly for him, it's like working at something he's not quite happy about, but with his best friend. When I mount a young horse for the first few times I scratch him, usually on the withers, so that he associates my weight on his back with something pleasurable.

BECOME AN IMPORTANT PERSON IN YOUR HORSE'S LIFE

After I have sized up a new horse in my mind I try to make myself count for something in his life. I start by introducing myself. I stand somewhere near him and watch him; I let him come up and sniff me. Then I begin to move about and also to make him change position. Sometimes this is easy, sometimes difficult. If he doesn't want to move I have to show him, though I'm not necessarily the boss in every sense of the word, I am taking the decision on this occasion.

When I worked three stallions at liberty in a group that included Templado, I allowed him a certain say in what we did. He was the wise stallion who influenced us all by his will, and I went along with it. I was more of an advisor during the proceedings even though in the end it was my decision: I suggested what we were going to work on, knowing full well that if Templado decided to take the other stallions back to the stable there would be some interesting negotiation! He was at the top of the hierarchy and I had to respect that. Templado was more determined than any other horse I have known, and because of that I allowed him privileges that perhaps I will never extend to another horse.

A FEW TIPS FOR COMMUNICATING

I commonly do the following and you may find they help:

- Place the palm of your hand on various parts of the horse's body while standing beside him—at a standstill and walking— and when mounted. Watch his reactions and try to read their meaning. Believe that the horse is telling you how he feels and try to listen to what he is saying.

- Try different movements of the hand in different places while standing beside him or when mounted: scratching with the tips of the fingers or in a circular movement, gentle at first. Watch and "listen"! People, who have little to do with horses, often pat them without any particular thought behind the action. In my experience horses do not like this, and it is therefore a waste of time. Persevere and concentrate your mind on giving your horse pleasure while you touch him. Vary the strength of the movement; you will soon discover what he likes.

Training sessions are so important because they establish the pleasure of working and being together, and this carries over into performances. Here Frédéric watches Mandarin from a bit of a distance before coming up to him, touching him, and allowing Mandarin to sniff him. Note Mandarin's beautiful relaxed head and nose muscles. You can see he's happy.

- Try speaking to your horse. It is not so much the words that are important but the tone of your voice and the body language that accompanies what you say. When you find something that appears to have a good effect, try to remember it and use it regularly when appropriate. If, for instance, you want to reassure your horse or praise him, say something as simple as "Good boy!" accompanied

by a rub on the withers; use the combination of tone and gesture that seems to have the best effect and stick to it.

I will sometimes walk with a young horse on a lead rope first, requesting he follow me. I stop and ask him to back up. I demonstrate to him how easy and pleasant it is to walk with me. Then I might try the same thing in a round pen at liberty. Once I have his attention I try stepping away or running a few steps. I watch to see if he follows and note the expression in his eyes. If he ignores me, I quietly put the lead rope on and try to recapture his attention by walking, stopping, and backing. I reward his attention with complimentary sounds.

We use our voices a lot but the words are combined with tone and also convey their meaning by the length of the word. "No, no, no, no," could be understood as a short word repeated and uttered with an air of admonishment, usually accompanied by a warning movement of the hand and arm. "Go-o-o-od boy," is a long soothing sound. I also use tongue "clucks" to add energy or impulsion to a movement, as I'm sure most people do.

But your voice is only one element of communication; as you become closer to the horse and more experienced, other elements gain in importance and the power of the mind gradually gains dominance over all.

Slow Ahead!

Magali relates her experience: "When I work with a new or a young horse I do everything in slow motion. Whether we are walking, trotting, cantering, or galloping, I make the horse work as slowly and quietly as I can. I speak to him in a calming, friendly way. I speak to him in language whose inflections would be understood by any mother speaking to her child. Quite often, I gently repeat '*Encore, encore*,' extending the vowels (or 'Once more, once more' might be better than 'Again, again' because of the long drawn-out vowels). Or I say, '*Voila! Voila bien!*' ('There's a good boy'), my voice drawn out like a caress.

Frédéric often spends time just watching the horses get used to their surroundings—here Mandarin is perhaps looking at his reflection in the water.

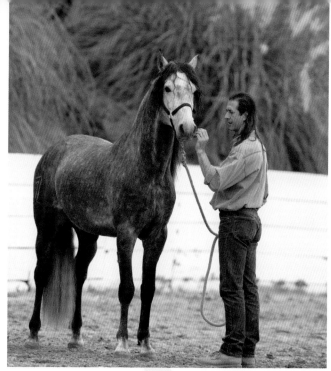

Lyrico is five years old and has lots of energy. Frédéric often works him on the longe in order to help control this energy and keep his attention. Here, the horse looks elsewhere as Frédéric tries to read him. Frédéric catches Lyrico's attention and moves him out while keeping contact with his eye. You can see Frédéric exercising some light tension to teach "giving way," and then backing Lyrico up with no tension at all on the halter.

"I try to make the horse conscious that he has four feet and that he has to place them carefully one in front of the other. In this way he develops his sense of balance and becomes aware of his body and the rhythm of his steps. Balance is central to all movement, for a horse just as it is for a rider, and the rider must not interfere with the horse's balance. It is only by doing everything slowly and calmly that one can develop this sense of balance and prepare for faster or more demanding work.

"With a mature horse my main preoccupation is to avoid all tension in his muscles while we work. Even before mounting, I explore his body with my eyes and hands and try to eliminate the least sign of tension in a muscle. When I am mounted, I explore his body with my mind and my own body movements, and often, I seem to get a message from some part of his body that there is a tense muscle. On occasion this reflects itself in a parallel part of my own body. By concentrated thought and gentle movements, by seeking perfect balance, I persuade the muscle to release its tension. If I don't do this, the tension could spread from one place all over the body, make the horse irritable, and give him a negative reaction to learning."

DEVELOPING "LONG" MUSCLES

"As I develop a horse, I try to ensure that he has what I call 'long' muscles," explains Magali. "These can only be formed when muscles are relaxed while they are working. If a muscle has tension then the horse will inevitably develop 'short' muscles. With experience one can see this quality just by looking at a horse. Horses with short muscles can have frequent physical problems and suffer from niggling complaints. People sell their horses because they get fed up with all the things that seem to go wrong and my experience is that this is often the reason.

"Horses working in tension do not develop harmonious muscles. I am proud when I see my horses: they all look like athletes because of their long, flexible, tension-free muscles and the way they work in harmony and support the horse's body mass and frame with grace and poise.

"I heard about an interesting parallel in the world of ballet: a young dancer was sent to London to a top ballet school. In his home country, his coach had concentrated on building up superb leg muscles, so that the boy could achieve astonishing jumps. However, the muscle

Magali on Dao practicing in costume at home in preparation for Equitana in Essen, Germany. One of Magali's main goals is to avoid all tension in the horse's muscles while they work together. Throughout her warm-up, and even when she moves on to practice difficult and demanding movements, like passage and piaffe, she remains attuned to Dao's body, watching for the smallest sign of tension so she can "persuade" the muscle to release and prevent the tension from spreading.

development in his upper legs was so exaggerated that it actually pulled him forward so that his point of balance was affected. An experienced physical trainer saw this and set out to relax and stretch the muscles. Within a short time, as photographs clearly showed, his stance had changed and his balance point had moved back. He could still do his amazing jumps, but he looked quite different and was subsequently taken on by the ballet company.

"When you find a horse with the right potential, but whose muscles have been badly built up, the only solution is to let him do nothing for a couple of months, allowing him to lose his muscle tone, and then start again building up his muscles properly. Owners sometimes sell a perfectly good horse because they tell me he is all screwed up, sometimes even aggressive. I know from looking at him that he has been worked in tension but I can see that he has good conformation and could turn out to be a really fine horse if his muscles were to be built up without tension, either mental or physical. Quite often it is one end of the horse—the front or the rear—that has been built up in the wrong manner so that he gives the appearance of being two different horses, one part well developed, and the other all wrong. This has happened to us a number of times and is occasionally a way of acquiring a good horse at a good price when the owner has run out of patience, refuses to try retraining him, and insists on selling!"

BODY LANGUAGE

"Whereas Frédéric has used his knowledge and experience to develop liberty acts," Magali continues. "I have concentrated on bringing certain horses to the highest standard of dressage. Most people do not necessarily want to compete but even so, should realize that the term 'dressage' covers the type of training that is essential for every horse that is to be ridden. If you only want to have a horse as a companion, it is a different matter, but as soon as you get into the saddle, other imperatives come into play: the horse can no longer see you unless he cranes his neck to either side, so body language, vital to communication when you are on foot, is no longer effective in the same way. Information to the horse is still conveyed partly by voice but principally through your seat, legs, hands, and balance.

"And it works the other way: when I am in the saddle I can feel the slightest tension in almost any muscle in the horse's body. I can, for instance, tell if the saddle is causing problems. As every rider knows, saddles frequently cause pain and trouble and some horses have much more sensitive backs than others. Mandarin's is so sensitive that I use one of three different saddles and sometimes I have to change the saddle every few days. Had he been ridden by someone unable to feel these tensions, he could have become a difficult horse to ride.

"When I feel a saddle might be causing trouble, I also try taking it off and riding without one. If the horse then goes well, I know that the saddle is the likely source of problems. I put the saddle back on and I can usually tell where it is hurting the horse because 'the hurt' is transmitted through to my hands, telling me where the muscle tension is. But if he's still showing pain when ridden bareback and there appears to be a problem in the spinal column or the muscles either side of it, there's no point in putting any saddle back on. So, I might ride without a saddle for a couple of months or until the problem goes away or has been treated.

"Of one thing there is no question: a saddle, a bit, the action of hands on the mouth, the weight of a person on the back, the pressure of the legs—all these are unnatural to a horse and can therefore create problems. With a young horse that you are starting, you must be particularly attentive to any sign of back pain and be ready and willing to change your schedule. For instance, you could go back to working in-hand for a time."

GIVE THE HORSE A "SAY"

I always watch to see what activity or game a horse likes and then I make a certain body movement to go with it; he soon associates the movement with that particular activity. I told you how Templado would go into a cabrade above me when I knelt on the ground. Magali told the story of Phoebus touching Gracioso on the rump with my whip and producing an immediate response (p. 39). When I provoke the activity by making the movement, I consider this subtly but significantly different from forcing a horse to learn something; it has become a matter of following up his pleasure, his choice. A new neural pathway is formed in an atmosphere free of stress or compulsion and soon becomes automatic.

On occasion, a horse will appear to have learned something and then suddenly forget it. Is this so strange? We are not foreign to this weakness ourselves. I just accept it; I don't become cross or feel despair but just return to the exercise, perhaps after a few days' rest.

Riding Mandarin without a saddle allows Magali to check for any tension in his very sensitive back. By rotating saddles as needed, Magali changes the pressure points created by the saddle and reduces the extreme tension of his back muscles. Here he is with a Stübben saddle made especially for him, which greatly improved his comfort and allowed him to move freely, as you can see by his piaffe in perfect balance. Magali is certain to encourage him to stretch and step under himself, continuing to develop his "long" muscles, even when warming up prior to competition. (See more about Mandarin on p. 146.)

Sometimes, after a period of work, I return to a horse and see from his attitude that he is less happy than he was before I worked with him, even though I had been under the impression that the session went well. It is almost as if he dislikes me a little and I have then to consider carefully what has caused it. There is always a reason for a change in a horse's attitude and it is up to us to discover it.

ESTABLISH LIMITS OF BEHAVIOR…AND RESPECT

I allow absolutely no biting or jostling: this is a rule that I start establishing with a young horse from the first day I work with him. In fact, with one that I do not know, I impose a strict limit as to how close he approaches me. No two horses are the same but as a guide I would suggest a distance of a forearm. Confidence breeds respect and vice versa. In liberty training, if there is mutual confidence between us, I can allow myself to tap the horse on his legs with my whip without causing him to run away—but only if my action is a justified reaction to something wrong or disobedient that he has done.

A common mistake is to do too much "snuggling up" to a horse from the beginning. You should keep the distance appropriate to the stage of your relationship. I don't immediately let a horse invade my space. Quite apart from the danger of being bitten, it puts you on the wrong footing. Once there is total confidence and respect in both directions it becomes another matter.

It is not easy to define rule making. It may seem from what I have said that there are few rules and that the horse is encouraged to take the initiative. However, it is the case that rules are not only essential but that the horse functions the better for accepting certain guidelines. Here is the crux of the situation: you must not impose unreasonable rules that the horse feels he cannot accept with a willing spirit.

Man has deprived the horse of his natural state; the horse has been dragged into the world of humans and therefore it is the foundation stone of our relationship that we earn his respect before anything else. He has lost his freedom but we can give him protection, security, and respect. In return, he will give us respect and affection and recognize the behavioral limits that we set together.

In order to become important to a horse, we cannot remain neutral. I have to impose laws and make it absolutely clear what is not allowed. At the same time, I know that horses often crave reassurance even more than liberty so I must provide this. I have to encourage this craving and convince them that I am the person to satisfy the need.

It has always amazed me how quickly a good chiropractor or osteopath convinces a horse that he is important to him. The horse understands in no time at all that the osteopath will relieve him of his aches and pains and therefore accepts him as a friend. This is why I think it is so important to spend time reassuring a horse and helping him relax rather than treating him with rewards. I often spend a quarter of an hour in the company of a horse, either in his stall or in the field, without asking anything of him. I just rub him gently and caress him and try to show him that there is all the time in the world; I am not going to rush him and I'm not going to make unreasonable demands.

Horses' Instinctive Appreciation of Justice

I think it is part of growing up that Phoebus has recently become more frisky and difficult. Suddenly he gives Guizo a nip. I give him a tap with my whip. He knows he shouldn't bite another horse and as long as I tap him with the right amount of strength, he will accept it; he will even put his head on my shoulder as if to say "I know, I know." But if he only "looks" as though he is going to bite another horse and I give him a sharp tap instead of a warning word, that is not fair and he knows it. He runs away and this time I have to make it up to him by going to him. Even after an hour's work I may still see in his eye that he is hurt and depressed.

The secret is to deploy the right amount of warning signals when I see a horse has something naughty in mind. "Don't even think about it," is a common enough warning between people and I have to find the equivalent for the horse, but it has to be one that he associates with his intention. He then says in effect, "Fair game."

When horses are in a field together, they will occasionally bite each other and if you are not there, there's nothing you can do about it. The hope is that by not stimulating aggression in your training and having a contented horse who enjoys his work, he will restrict himself to the odd friendly nip and not do any great harm.

People Are Not Fence Posts!

Whatever happens I never allow a horse to rub himself against me. People are not fence posts: even when afraid, the horse must not be allowed to knock against me or tread on my feet, let alone oblige me to jump out of his way. The problem is, how do you impose these rules without breaking all the precepts I have been laying down? You do it with firmness but without getting angry.

When I am working with a horse at liberty and he comes too close, I gently but firmly push him away by placing the point of the whip I carry, on his shoulder. If he is frightened I have to show him that I appreciate his fear but that it does not give him the excuse to penetrate my personal "bubble" of space. Take note: everything I describe is a reaction to the horse's unacceptable behavior, not an unprovoked action.

GAME-PLAYING

You can develop your relationship with the horse through game-playing. As always when using terms invented to describe human activity there has to be an effort of the imagination. Take "dancing" for instance. The essence of a brilliant performance by two people is not just that they do the steps perfectly and in time to the music but that they add an emotional quality that lifts the performance into another realm. I strive to achieve this emotional element with my horses. We both have to be totally concentrated on what we are doing. I can suggest games and sometimes the horse will show me he wants to try something. Neither of us is totally in control. In my performances I never know for sure what my horses will decide to do. My job is to create the background, the mood, the feeling of security, and a readiness to respond and to reward them with my approval. The "dances" are not always the same. In fact, they are never the same two times running and at any time a horse can come up with something new, unexpected, and wonderful.

Knowing how to ask a horse to play is all-important. You want him to respect what you ask of him without balking or getting upset.

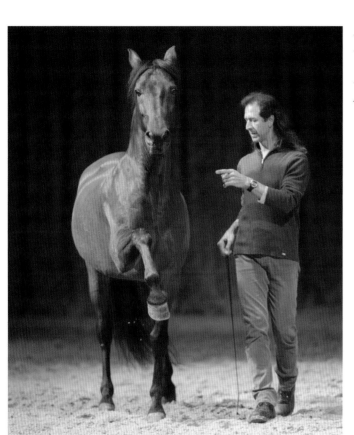

Delirio doing the Spanish walk. Frédéric concentrates on the quality of the movement as Delirio concentrates on his physical effort. The result is the beginnings of a "dance."

You want him to remain willing and attentive. I find that when a horse is ready to play he gives his assent and cooperates. You must wait for this moment so you can start with simple requests that will get a positive response, then you build on that. If the horse has a second of doubt you have to reassure, not press ahead. In this way, he is allowed to feel he is in control of himself. I am convinced that in the end it saves time waiting for horses to say when they are ready for the next advance.

Magali adds: "I always interleave periods of hard work with pleasurable games or walks and relaxing moments. Games for us often include cabrades and rolling, which a lot of our horses enjoy and think of as rewards. You have to be clear in your mind what is 'work' and what is 'play,' and know it will vary from horse to horse. With Mandarin, I often break off training and go for a trail ride to give him a nibble and a stroll. My father also taught me to introduce little bits of more difficult work, like a piaffe, during a walk in the country, preferably at a place that the horse really likes so that he builds up an association of the work and pleasurable feelings.

"I have a special game with Dao. He wants me to touch his ear so he looks around and then stares at me. If I don't react he pushes his head toward me, still staring intently. I touch his face and he pushes more. I touch his leg and so on until he has had enough and stops. I then touch his ear and we have had our little intimate exchange."

Variety Is the Spice of Life

I try to vary the activities as much as possible so that the horses do not become bored. As with a person, when boredom creeps in, concentration reduces. I quite often suggest jumping over small obstacles, but I never go on too long. You must avoid the danger of the horse developing a negative association with any particular exercise. I often adopt an almost dilettante approach so that the horse does not feel pressured. To go on with the same exercise relentlessly can only do harm. I sometimes suggest a game and then leave it for a while, returning as if by accident later on. I try to give the horse the feeling that it is not of any great importance and that I am not interfering with his freedom and enjoyment, yet in returning every now and again, I can persuade him that it's a good idea to add the game to his repertoire. It must always be centered round play and not become work with constraint.

Magali and Bandolero like to practice outside the arena. The best place to teach the Spanish walk is when going out for a walk—the idea being to get the horse out of a work frame of mind and into one of pleasure.

This goes for the rider, too: Frédéric on Famoso, Estelle on Guizo, and Magali on Bandolero enjoy a sunset gallop.

I've tried a number of approaches and I am now more than ever convinced that the basis of all my work must be to create pleasure in play and freedom from stress. I usually avoid the word "work" because in our human world the word often has a negative connotation. With patience, time, and gentleness everything can be transformed into play; from the most advanced dressage steps to the most carefree ride in the woods. By transforming what might be deemed work into enjoyable play, the horse grows like a child and at the same time comes closer to us.

One Caution on "Play"

Unfortunately, the word "play" has become modish and is often used to describe something other than a shared, pleasurable experience. There is always the danger that it is a game to the rider and not to the horse. Watch carefully to see that the horse is not just submitting to becoming a plaything. A proper game requires mutual respect so the rules must be accepted by both parties. Some of our horses like being chased on foot and then giving chase themselves; Mandarin likes running alongside me; Phoebus adores playing with the whip and finding where it has been hidden; Phoebus and Paulus love playing together, as do Gracil and Guizo.

Frédéric and Fasto playing together on the beach in Malibu, California, after a long but successful week of Cavalia performances.

Games properly set up and used can be an aid to motivation, concentration, and memory, and help understanding between you and your horse to grow. They can also be used to push the horse to do more than he has achieved until this point. Learning to go beyond what he has already achieved brings an increase in pleasure and develops intelligence. This in turn enables the horse to better control his fears and to acquire a higher standard of physical and mental health.

Through the use of games a horse goes on discovering new and better ways to learn and, in doing so, comes closer in intelligence to that of human beings. The "distance" between us shrinks, and our pleasure in the horse's company grows. With Templado I sometimes felt that he had come to resemble me and I, him. Magali has the same strange feeling with Dao. Of course it's a fantasy, but when the fantasy has passed, the feeling has not altogether evaporated. We have begun to identify with each other.

EDUCATING FOALS AND YOUNG HORSES

Very early on I begin to spend time with a newly born foal to accustom him to the feel of my hands. I touch and caress him all over so that he accepts it as part of his life, just as, to give an unfortunate parallel, a child who is beaten when young assumes that beating is part of its life. Depending on how fast the foal develops and it may be at one month or three months old, I put a loose rope around his neck. At first this is for only a few seconds and I do not pull at all. I start by going with any movement he makes so that there is absolutely no feeling of resistance.

When he is used to this, I wait until he sets off in a direction, then exert the tiniest pressure to one side as we move along together and immediately release the pressure when he makes the smallest concession. The object is always to establish a compromise: he wants to go north and I want to go east—we should end up going northeast. It is really only commonsense and I think that many sensitive people who read this will have done the same thing without my instruction. After all, isn't that what we should all strive for as couples: to compromise and go northeast?

Whenever we have a new foal we start playing games when he is still very young. I am always suggesting little games to my foals with the sole object of instilling in them the love of playing, and this helps greatly in keeping up their excitement and interest in the process of learning. Even if the foal does not understand immediately what I expect of him he gradually does so, as I gently and repeatedly suggest

Two sons of Perdigon, Guizo and Gracil were born in the same year, often work together, and get on extremely well. Here Frédéric introduces parts of the show to them, and they all enjoy "playing" together.

what I want. This allows him to feel that he takes charge of the situation; I listen and follow his wishes.

I generally start riding or even mounting young horses when they are three years old. Before that I might lean on a horse but not apply my full weight. When I do mount it will only be for a moment, and then I dismount and see how the new experience has affected him. When I get off I give him a scratch in his favorite place so he associates the new sensation of weight bearing with a pleasant feeling. The act of mounting, which is a form of constraint on the horse, introduces a bridge toward the concept of work and confuses the two ideas (work and play) in a good way. When it comes to doing serious work the horse will already be well disposed toward the idea; it will not be a sudden nasty shock of something new that is completely unrelated to play and relaxation.

Horses in the racing world are saddled and ridden at such a young age that they are often worn out when they are still young. Each horse develops at a different rate and hurrying the pace only leads to trouble later. Although I start mounting a horse for short rides when he is three, it is then only at most once a week. I do not think, as some do, training has to be "completed" by the age of four. Some horses are late developers and in such cases it is best to slow your schedule accordingly, even delaying certain steps for months.

I wish I could always start with a foal but sometimes it is not possible. We have to buy mature horses and even ones that have been trained by others. For instance, I once bought a fine looking horse for *Cavalia,* and I noticed immediately that he did not like anyone entering his stall so I examined him very carefully and found a nasty scar on his tongue that could only have resulted from a vicious tug on the bit. So we spent time each day with him in his stall, not doing anything particular, just being with him; soon he was more welcoming and I think he will turn out all right. A horse never forgets ill treatment but, just as with people, the effects can be softened and his confidence built up again slowly. Of course, it was my responsibility never to break trust and let him down.

A mature horse that has experienced training elsewhere is often inflexible and much slower to learn new ways because his development has been channeled down a narrow path. When I can bring up a horse from birth and use the concept of play from the beginning, by the time he is mounted for the first time learning for him is easy in all directions.

In fact, he will seem eager to learn new things. Learning is as much a pleasure for him as for me.

Set Problems to Develop Curiosity and Intelligence

Horses are by nature curious. Alas, how is it that so many riders discourage this natural instinct? The appetite for discovery that can turn into a real thirst for knowledge, if it is nurtured, is all too often killed off at a young age. I not only allow curiosity, I encourage it; far from putting limits to it, I stimulate it. To do this I set my horses a series of little challenges that constantly exercise their intelligence and give them a taste for experimentation. For example, I'll place a bowl of grain out of reach unless they put their front feet on a cube just inside the door of the stall. Magali has been hiding her whip for Quelam to find and he clearly enjoys the challenge—and usually succeeds in meeting it. On another occasion I might hide some grain in the back of an open horse trailer that I park in a paddock. It doesn't usually take the horses turned out in the paddock long to discover the treasure, and this has the added advantage of teaching young horses to enter a horse trailer without fear. When horses are allowed the opportunity to find the solution to a problem they are delighted, and it makes them even more eager to find solutions to problems in the future.

As is so often the case, the chief enemy of curiosity is fear. Gracil, for example, was terrified of the bright spots on the ground caused by sunlight piercing the branches of trees. If I had forced him to step into these areas of light he would certainly have dug in his heels and refused. What I did instead was to let him explore this phenomenon by himself. I encouraged him and when he finally put a foot tentatively into a patch of light I was quick to congratulate him. (I tell you more about Gracil on p. 133.)

When I am mounted, I do show a little more firmness in a parallel situation, but I always allow the horse the chance to hesitate and work out the solution to the problem for himself and thus make his own decision.

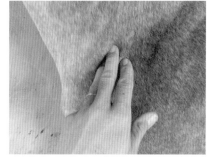

When using pressure to ask a horse to "give way" and move back, as Frédéric does, position your finger between the horse's shoulder and the neck where there is a sort of depression. Never push enough to cause hurt or the horse will become tense and could react aggressively.

Templado on the longe line warming up for a photo shoot. Even though Templado is not young here, he benefits from the gentle exercise and Frédéric's nearness, which helps deal with any fears or insecurities he might have in the open field.

The Importance of "Giving Way"

One of the first lessons I teach a new horse is to "give in" to the tension of the longe or lead line. It's a subtle but important difference: you are trying to teach him *not to pull* but instead *to give way*. If you attach a horse for the first time to something that is immovable, such as a ring on the wall of his stall, he will almost certainly exhibit excessive fear and leap violently backward trying to escape—but it is perfectly possible to overcome this fear. If he exhibits the same violent reaction when you are holding him, you can and must give way to him, exerting no more than a gentle, calm resistance, until the horse *gives way* back. Similarly, I teach all my horses to move backward by the simple pressure of a finger placed on their chest—*giving way* when asked.

It is common practice nowadays to work a young horse in a round pen but this can have results that are often misinterpreted. The horse is worked under stress and finally comes to the trainer who thinks the horse has "given in" to him and will henceforth do what is asked of him. All too often the horse is frightened and because he can't escape, he capitulates like a zebra trapped by hyenas. He simply resigns and the flame is extinguished. The spark of enjoyment in learning must be nurtured, not dampened, and this can only be done slowly. I prefer to start a young horse on a longe line; there is less likelihood of confusion and panic. He learns to be near you and it is easier to reassure him and desensitize him to his fears.

The stress of certain "speed training" methods can produce measurable damage because the horse learns to be obedient by the clever manipulation of the trainer and without the horse's voluntary participation as part of the process. The same phenomenon has been observed in children who have been exposed to violence and stress. We are committing a grave mistake when we use these alien methods on a horse. They simply resign themselves and something in their personality is destroyed. In my opinion, it is abuse on our part.

When I see a trainer put a young horse in a ring and drive him round relentlessly until the horse gives up and comes to him, I think the person has lost the opportunity of being on the right footing with the horse. Instead, if longeing is done properly the first time, the horse can stop after a few circles and come to you in the middle. You praise him and reward him with scratching and rubbing in the places you know he likes. You hope he will say to himself, "It's okay, I'll be your friend." This stage of training should be successfully concluded before attempting liberty work. In other words, you have first to establish the mutual confidence that elementary longe work produces.

OUR UNDERSTANDING OF THE HORSE'S MIND

There have been many trainers who have contributed to the understanding of the extraordinary relationship of man and horse. There will be many more and the process will continue as long as there are people and horses. I think we are still at an early stage in this development. It was set back by man usually taking the apparently easy route to control the horse over the centuries—that of domination. Training by domination can and has achieved much, because of man's cleverness and the strength and adaptability of the animal. An automobile with horsepower measured in hundreds allows man to achieve impressive speeds and execute complex maneuvers, but even one "horsepower" has allowed him to multiply his strength and effectiveness, to travel distances at a speed impossible on foot, and to execute the most complex dressage figures.

But none of this has necessarily increased our understanding of the horse's mind and how to communicate with him from the standpoint of being just another animal with different abilities and other contributions to the game of life. Could it possibly be a result of the beliefs of some of the world's religions that man is celebrated as a creature far superior to all others? In the Judeo-Christian religion, God supposedly created Man after he had created all the other animals and gave Man dominion over them. It hardly needs saying that Man has abused this gift, if gift you believe it was.

The Six Golden Principles of Training

We arrive late in the afternoon at a new venue where we are to take part in a performance. The drivers of the horse van are tired, as well as are all the handlers who want to unload the horses and clean up as soon as possible so they can go for their dinner. This is the moment that Gracil chooses not to leave the van.

Gracil enters horse trailers and vans like a lamb but is sometimes less than eager about leaving; perhaps he needs to be reassured that the ramp is going to support him! It would be so easy in a situation like this to forget my principles, speak harshly to him, and maybe give his halter a hearty tug. If I were to do this, I can tell you, he would let me know the next time we did a liberty number together, and it might take some days for me to recover the perfect trust that currently exists between us, and which I rely on to perform the acts we do in my shows. I cannot abandon our principles without paying heavily for it. In a case like this I just have to tell the driver and handlers to go away for a while, and then in a state of peace and calm, I give Gracil the time and reassurance he needs and finally lead him quietly down the ramp.

THE SIX GOLDEN PRINCIPLES

What then are the six principles on which Magali and I base our work?

1   To foster a more equal relationship, based on trust and respect, in which horse and man learn from each other.

2   Never to adopt "standard" or inflexible methods of training but to recognize that each horse develops as an individual and reacts differently to the same stimulus.

3   To reduce stress as well as to become a safe, trusted "haven" for the horse.

4   Always to be patient and never push too fast or too insistently— and on the other hand, not to allow the horse to get bored.

5   Never to use force or become angry.

6   To establish a more "natural" form of communication—that is, to further new methods.

PRINCIPLE ONE
To foster a more equal relationship, based on trust and respect, in which horse and man learn from each other.

I believe we can forge a new kind of relationship with a horse, one that is based on a greater degree of equality than most people have thought possible. Horses themselves form very close relationships that can last for life. I want the same: I want to reach the stage where they don't drive me from their space and I don't drive them from mine. I have to convince them that the space belongs to both of us. The best way to explain this belief is to talk about the liberty acts where I have to put my beliefs to the test in front of audiences. When I come into the ring with loose horses, I have an idea of what I think we may be doing together but the horses may well have different ideas, and I never know exactly how the evening will turn out. Occasionally, it is not just the audience that is amazed and delighted, but me.

During these liberty acts I even allow the horses to take up the position vis-a-vis each other that makes them most comfortable. Of course, I vary the degree of influence to get my way. For instance, in the act I do with three Lusitanos, I let them choose who wants to be in the middle but once established, they have to keep that order. When I do the same act with the much younger Friesians, Phoebus and Paulus, together with Guizo, a Pure Spanish (PRE) horse, I persuade Guizo to be between the other two since this avoids potential trouble when the Friesians become overexcited or decide that it would be fun to have a brotherly nip.

The horses love munching grass so Frédéric likes to teach them the "reverence" in the field. Since they first associate the movement with getting a good mouthful of grass, when asked to do it in the arena, they are very willing.

Lancelot Plays to the Audience

I remember one occasion when I was performing with Lancelot, one of our Pure Spanish horses. I had already entered the ring; Lancelot followed but did not at first see me. He peered about and after improvising some steps, clearly playing to his audience, went into a perfect cabrade. Then, to my astonishment, he lay down and rolled, something he had never done in public and very rarely while working with me alone; he is a rather nervous horse and to lie down

Lancelot is an extraordinary performer because of his energy, which communicates itself to the audience. He does explosive voltes and cabrades (like the expressive one shown here), and then often rushes to Frédéric to bury his head in Frédéric's hands for a "calming session." He has had lots of standing ovations for his performances, and while he loves public reaction, he is occasionally overwhelmed and loses his nerve.

is frightening for him. The audience applauded, Lancelot got up, did another cabrade and then, as if playing with his fear, lay down and rolled again. The audience made even more noise so he repeated the whole performance. Then he saw me, got up, raced over toward me, did yet another cabrade and stuck his head into my arms for affectionate recognition. It was a magic moment for the public as much as for me because it was absolutely clear to everyone that he had received no instructions from me: it was an act of his own invention. And now it is part of his repertoire! He continues to invent new games for my pleasure and that of the public.

Three Stallions Invent a Number

On another occasion I was doing a number with the three stallions Aetes, Fasto, and Templado in Essen, Germany. At the end of the act the horses galloped across the ring toward me but, as they were stopping and preparing for a cabrade, Aetes turned around and galloped back to the other side of the ring (about 65 feet away) where there was a box. There he turned again, put one front leg on the box and performed a perfect jambette. At the same time the other two stallions reared up into a wonderful cabrade. When Aetes saw this he galloped over to join the other two. Then they came toward me, all three content. The jambette had made up for the disobedience and Aetes knew it. This number was a total surprise to me—like a gift of joy.

Templado Comes Back to Fetch Me

Toward the end of this same show the three stallions were heading toward the exit gate. The man in charge of the gate, thinking it was the end of the number, opened it and they all rushed through. But then Templado, noticing that I wasn't in front of them as was my custom, reckoned something must be wrong, and turned around. Just when I thought I was going to find myself all alone in the arena looking fairly stupid, Templado came back to me at full gallop, stopped in front of me, and made a magnificent cabrade. I ran toward the exit with Templado following me, and of course the crowd was beside itself. No doubt most people thought the idea had been worked out beforehand instead of being the spontaneous improvisation that it actually was!

This is Aetes' favorite act: a jambette on the box—only here Frédéric is sharing his pleasure (it is part of the plan rather than Aetes' improvisation!)

A Disappointed Spectator

Indeed after the show a horse trainer came up to me and said, "Magnificent! But I didn't see you give the cue for one of your three horses to go to a box and do that jambette, or when the horses ran out of the ring and one came back to fetch you."

"But I didn't give them a cue," I replied proudly.

The man was visibly taken aback and disappointed. How could

I be a proper horse trainer if I was not totally in control? Well, these moments when I am not totally in control, when the horses on their own initiative do something spectacular either to please the audience or me—or for the sheer joy of doing something without compulsion—however you wish to interpret it, they are the ones I live for.

Templado's Trust

On another occasion I was performing a number with Templado in an arena in Stockholm—about 265 by 130 feet (80 by 40 meters) large—in front of a colossal audience of some 50,000 spectators. The Swedes can be famously tricky to please: I have seen a number by another trainer received at the end in total silence. This made a lasting impression on me and I had no desire to be the next victim.

As we finished Templado and I made our bow to the audience, and then I ran for the exit. Whether it was because he did not hear me through the applause of so many people or he did not see me leave, I don't know, but when I reached the gate I turned to see that Templado was still down on one knee in his "reverence," all alone in the middle of this immense arena.

What on earth was happening? Was something wrong with him, I wondered? Before I could do anything he looked about him, rose to his feet, turned full circle in a kind of waltzing, galloping step, his beautiful mane flying about his head as he pirouetted, and then, not seeing me, clearly decided that I had not yet given him the okay to leave—so he dropped down into another "reverence." I rushed back to him across the arena, deeply moved by his act of trust, and caressed him. The audience was ecstatic. This time I ran off and he galloped out behind me.

The Right Path Is Never Smooth

Moments like these convince me that I am on the right track and moving in the right direction. They confirm my belief that with patience and understanding we can forge a new relationship with horses and achieve more than even I had thought possible and achieve it without constraint or domination. But to do so we must have the conviction to

Templado, Fasto, and Aetes go down into a "reverence" at the Salon du Cheval in Paris, 2001. (No grass but pleasant memories.)

see us through all the setbacks and disappointments. Every day, and this is still true for myself, there are moments of disappointment and self-doubt. It is not an easy path and it never will be.

Principle Two
Never to adopt "standard" or inflexible methods of training but to recognize that each horse develops as an individual and reacts differently to the same stimulus.

As with People, So with Horses

It is commonplace to say and to believe that every person is different from everyone else. The same is true for horses and the difference between each of them is as great as the difference between humans. As with humans, many characteristics are decided by hereditary makeup, the rest depending on upbringing and relationships with other horses and with humans.

When I explain to people that I am not in the business of putting forward yet another training method, they quite naturally want to know what method I *do* favor. As usual, there is no simple answer: there are lots of reasonable methods that individuals have developed over the years, though you have to apply all of them with sensitivity and without losing sight of the principles I am trying to instill—that is, of course, if you are won over to our approach.

In dealing with other people we learn to be aware of their wishes and their reactions to what we say and do. Likewise, we can learn to read horses, to be aware of their wishes and reactions, but the language is different so we have to learn it first. When people find themselves dealing with horses, all too often they ignore this obvious truth and throw commonsense out the window. They follow some method they have been taught or heard about and apply it without any attention to the horse's reaction. They make no effort to gauge whether the horse likes what they are trying to do or not. Put yourself in the horse's position. Would you care to be treated like this? To treat another human being in a preconceived manner, without any care for its effect on him or her, might be considered autistic behavior. Is it any different when dealing with a horse?

In conclusion, I would add that Linda Tellington-Jones' method of reading horses is the best I have come across.

The Dangers of Anthropomorphism

I find that the more I understand about horses, the more I avoid the dangers of anthropomorphism. In fact, horses share many similar traits and emotions with humans. It's just that we have to use *our* words to describe them, and they may, in fact, be subtly different in what they describe. "Love" and "friendship" are, potentially, real traps. Did Templado *love* me? I would hesitate using the word. He certainly *needed* me. An emotion that, in my opinion, horses do not share with us is compassion (and one might say the same of children, whom they resemble in many ways).

One also has to be particularly careful of interpreting physical traits like yawning in a human context. People laugh when a horse yawns, but it is no laughing matter; it means something quite different and usually is an effort to relieve stress. A horse that appears to smile is usually smelling something and not enjoying a joke. There is only one way to avoid these sort of mistakes and that is to acquire knowledge about horses' mannerisms through reading and experience.

Developing Intelligence and Individuality

Magali describes one rule that applies to our treatment of any horse. "It is our duty to develop curiosity and intelligence," she says. "If you apply inflexible methods of training, how can you possibly fulfill this duty? There are trainers who have said that they do not think the horse is an intelligent animal. This claim tells you more about the person who made it than about horses. People quite often say to us, 'Your horses are of above-average intelligence.' No, we tell them, we make it a priority, right from the start of a relationship with each horse, to develop his natural curiosity. We allow and encourage any quirky behavior because the individuality of the horse is often expressed through his little idiosyncrasies. Try to erase these and you squash the horse's personality. Mandarin, for example, loves playing with a big ball and can go on almost indefinitely. I can tell you, he is better at dribbling and playing with the ball than a lot of soccer players! He pirouettes with it trapped between his hind legs, he hits it with his nose at a gallop, and kicks it forward with a front hoof.

"On one occasion I was distributing grain to the stalls. One of the horses was still out in the paddock but, knowing he was returning soon, I put his grain in his feed bin. A little later I was surprised to hear the sound of a horse's footsteps in the aisle but thought nothing of it since there were no other sounds of the sort you might expect if a stallion is walking about the barn loose. Then I discovered that the horse I had heard was Bandolero, who had opened the lock on his stall, wandered down to the empty box stall, pulled open the door, walked in, eaten the grain, and then returned to his own stall, adopting a touching look of innocence! Bandolero is in fact a charming horse who has to make up his own mind about things. If he doesn't want to do something, I have to put him through a whole cycle of games before he accepts it. But as this story shows, he is also very determined once he has decided he will do something." (Find out more about Bandolero on p. 156.)

Our "Methods"

If Magali and I can be said to use any particular method in our training it is the use of games and liberty work, and never forgetting that everything we use in the development of the horse's intelligence and individuality must be pleasurable to him. This is the legacy of Templado and is the engine that "drags" training forward. Playing games allows the horse to influence decisions because he has to think and, with experience on our part, we can begin to tell what he is thinking. Liberty work, apart from many other benefits, gives him the confidence that he is not being forced to do anything against his will. So both games and "free work" afford us the opportunity of watching the horse make decisions and of seeing how each horse reacts to the unexpected.

In order to allow the horse to develop his full potential, you will of course have to take the sort of risks that we humans take with other humans, but as long as you work in an ambiance of pleasurable activity, mistakes are not serious. Like children who are well taught, horses who are allowed to play and explore their curiosity soon appear

Frédéric with Guizo: obedience without restraint—just the joy of doing something together. Guizo looks for a little comfort in the practice ring.

more intelligent than those who are subjected to conventional training along fixed lines aimed at standard accomplishments. To dominate the will of a horse and to stifle initiative is, however kindly meant, a cruel deprivation—and all too commonplace.

Each Horse Has His Favorite Game

I like to reward a horse who has done good work by allowing him to play his favorite game. I soon learn which games each horse prefers and it is not difficult to enter into the fun of it. For instance, I might run away from him as fast as I can, knowing that he will enjoy the chase. What is more, I often interleave games with hard work on an exercise like the "reverence," the bowing movement that is arduous and requires a lot of effort to do.

As I mentioned before, Aetes, one of my oldest horses, likes to get up on his box (the wooden cube) on the stage and do a jambette for the fun of it. He will even come up to me and gently nibble my chin. I allow him to do this and when he does it during a show the

Frédéric getting a "bizou"—a kiss—from Aetes at the Salon du Cheval in Paris, 2001. While the crowd always loves it, Aetes doesn't do it to please the audience. The stallion discovered "bizous" when he was very young, and it's his way of seeking comfort and relief from the stress of the show, and feeling safe and close to Frédéric.

public thinks that it is as a result of long training. Not a bit of it! Aetes thought of the idea himself, and by permitting him this pleasure, I help to reduce the stress of the performance.

Templado, after a training session in which he was asked for more concentration than usual, would come up to me and do a magnificent cabrade as an expression of his own pleasure. Allowing him to share it with me was his reward—and it was very important for him to learn that extra effort brought such a reward. Fasto needs to gallop a lot during a performance so I have to take this into account, whereas Templado, when he was getting on in years, would be tired out and unhappy with too much effort.

My horses often show me great affection but this is only because I have won their respect and confidence over a long period. I do not allow them to overstep the mark. My responsibility is to make each horse as relaxed and free from stress as possible and I have never to forget for one moment that each one is an individual and has his own likes and dislikes.

"Acting on" rather than "Reacting to" My Wishes

A typical problem that I might encounter when training a young horse is the moment when I introduce the big wooden box or cube. Left alone the horse will go up to it, paw it with a foot, sniff it, and after a short time show no fear, but if I ask him to approach it, his natural instinct to resist pressure causes stress and raises doubts. The answer is, therefore, to create a relaxed atmosphere, without tension and without making heavy demands. I try to encourage the animal to think for himself and "act on" rather than "react to" my wishes. This also helps me discover the individual characteristics of each horse and adapt my approach to dealing with them.

The fact that my horses feel at ease and relaxed during instruction is to them a far greater reward than all the carrots in the world. Quite often I do nothing at all for a time; I just enjoy their company and they, mine. I can assure you, this feeling of shared contentment is something they are aware of, and it is very reassuring for them. The little games I suggest to my young horses have the sole object of instilling in them the love of play, and this helps greatly in maintaining their excitement and interest in the learning process. Even if the horse does not understand immediately what I expect of him, he gradually does so, as I gently and repeatedly suggest what I want. This allows him to feel that he takes charge of the situation, and that I listen and follow *his* wishes.

Magali agrees: "I never have long sessions of work without introducing periods of play. My aim is to make the sessions a pleasure for both of us. I have to discover what amuses and entertains each horse for no two are the same. I have told you about Mandarin's love of playing with the large ball: sometimes we both chase it and after a few minutes of this 'horse play,' he is more relaxed and ready to go on with work.

"Another of my horses has a tendency to be stiff. After a work session, I go for a walk with him and every so often tap him on one side of the neck or the other, so that he looks around to see what I want and in doing so bends his neck to the right and to the left. It is a mild sort of game but by the end of a short walk he is quite clearly more relaxed and flexible.

"As I've said before, horses often have a sense of naughtiness, something akin to a sense of humor. It is one way in which they express their character and individuality. I firmly believe this should be nurtured and not suppressed. Most people seem to have the idea that any quirkiness should be ironed out. Would they do this with their own child? I doubt it."

Working "with Pleasure" and Working "under Constraint"

The trouble with a lot of riding methods or "systems" is that we have inherited them through a long tradition of military horsemanship that focused on removing any problems between the soldier and his mount. "Flattening" the problems might have been a more apt word because the training was based more on the use of force than of cooperation. Armies needed a quick effective method that was inevitably authoritarian and generally did not consider the feelings of the horse. It had to be the same method for everyone and every horse.

People like my father and grandfather who worked their farms with horses, day in and day out, never received any formal training and would have made no claims to being wonderful riders. And yet, in their way their approach was much more flexible, and they had the ability to acknowledge and respond to the different characteristics of each horse.

In these pictures of Mandarin galloping and playing at liberty, you can see the engagement of his hind legs and the flexibility of his loins, which helps achieve the "lightness" at the front of the horse desired in dressage. The challenge with him is to watch and understand him at liberty and so Frédéric and Magali know how to control his explosion of energy and natural ability when mounted. Magali's lovely canter demonstrates how their methods are succeeding with this exuberant and talented horse.

Of course, in order to become a good rider, a good basic technique is indispensable, including a safe seat, calm, strong legs and good, gentle hands. Without being able to "sit into his seat" properly, the rider cannot hope to effectively pass on his thoughts and wishes to the horse. But even these are not enough. A rider must be able to adjust his instructions according to the horse's reactions. Without this ability, even the best rider will act as a "brake" on his horse's development.

Learning from a Riding "Master" but Remaining Flexible

Methods and teachers can be aids to becoming a good rider; a good master opens our minds and helps us to understand what we are doing and what is possible. But in the end, it is experience coinciding with a receptive mind that makes the rider. I sometimes see pupils of this or that well known instructor who blindly reproduce exercises they have been taught. They do not have sufficient understanding of why they are doing them or where an exercise is taking them, so they cannot adapt to problems met along the way. This is to apply a method with one's eyes closed. You have to keep your critical faculties about you all the time.

Quite often we can take the advice of a master as a starting point. It is then up to each one of us to find our own solution and customize it for each horse. For instance, the famous movie horse trainer I introduced earlier in the book, Corky Randall, recommended that in order to attract the attention of a horse at liberty, I tap him on the thigh with my whip. If a student took this as an immutable instruction it could result in a disaster—and I have witnessed a few. I have seen horses become aggressive after being subjected to so-called *gentle* methods, and I have seen them become bored. Through repetitive, mindless training, a horse may simply "shut down" and go through his paces like an automaton. Tapping a horse on the thigh does indeed work with the majority of horses, but not with all of them. There are always horses who are so frightened of the whip that the use of it distracts their attention from the job at hand. Anyway, it's simply not worth insisting in this way. There are lots of methods of attracting a horse's attention, snapping your fingers or breaking into a run beside them being only a couple.

To sum up: there is no one method that can be applied to every horse. The more experienced you are, the more you may favor a particular system or way of training, but you still have to be prepared to adjust it to each individual horse and to continue doing so as the horse develops. Remember, you do not treat every person you meet in the same way, nor do you treat someone in the same way forever, as long as you know him or her. Why then treat horses inflexibly?

Training Horses Based on Nature

When a horse is raised in a herd he is already "being trained" as a matter of course. If a foal bothers his mother or another member of the herd unreasonably, the adult will commonly raise a hind leg and hold it in the air. If the foal goes on being tiresome, he might get a kick. Next time he's a pest, the adult only has to raise a leg and the foal desists; he knows what is coming his way if he continues.

Similarly, if I want to stop bad behavior, I might say, "No, no, no, no," at the same time raising my hand in a warning gesture. The second time, I repeat the "No! No! No! No!" with a slightly more urgent tone and my gesture is more authoritative. The third time, I repeat the process but give the horse a sharp tap with my whip or crop, enough to get the message across that he will be a happier horse without getting that tap. Thereafter, I may only have to raise my crop with the same air of authority and the horse will desist. There is a huge void between this approach and that of relying on inflexible technical solutions.

Different breeds have different sensitivities: Lusitanos are particularly sensitive and I cannot use any harshness with them as it would damage our relationship, which is based on complete trust and respect. Friesians are less sensitive so I can be a little firmer, but I have to be very careful not to go too far. I am only talking about a degree or two; overdo it and the horse will let me know the next day, if not at the time.

Orchestral Conductor?

The problem is that stallions are huge powerful creatures with enough strength to crush a human being. When I am working with three boisterous young stallions in a liberty act it is potentially a dangerous undertaking, and I am like the conductor of an orchestra—except that horses are stronger than the average cellist! I have to keep all this strength and enthusiasm in control without putting a damper on the very qualities that make the performance so captivating.

When I am working with the two young brothers, Paulus and Phoebus, the latter can get overexcited and come too close to me. If I overdo the gestures I use to make him keep his distance, he might gallop off to the other side of the arena, or at least some distance away. When he does this I have to make sure I am calm myself and then call him back. When he returns, I caress him and we "make up" before continuing.

Or, Tightrope Walker?

As mentioned earlier in the book, Phoebus loves to retrieve my whip from the ground and bring it to me or even chase me with it in his

Phoebus and Paulus came to Frédéric and Magali when they were eight months old, and Frédéric and Magali played with them as a pair from the start. Here, Paulus discovers the box (and likes it!) and the two take their first air trip.

There's always time for a contented moment in the paddock and to play together after a day's work.

At one-and-a-half years old, Phoebus and Paulus played with Frédéric, learning to lie down in confidence and with pleasure, and prepared to join Cavalia. And they have a good time, romping together in Portugal when the were about three. Frédéric has always watched their play and observed the way their relationship changes as they grow and develop. When they were very young, Phoebus was the more forward of the two and called the tune. Then, Paulus began to build his strength and there was a period of some conflict and sparring. You can see Paulus exhibiting the flehmen response, proof of his maturation and ascent into "stallion-hood." At three years old, the stallions have achieved an equilibrium and can happily swap roles. The always do things together and it is amusing to see how very often, if one of them should look to the left, for example, the other will follow suit.

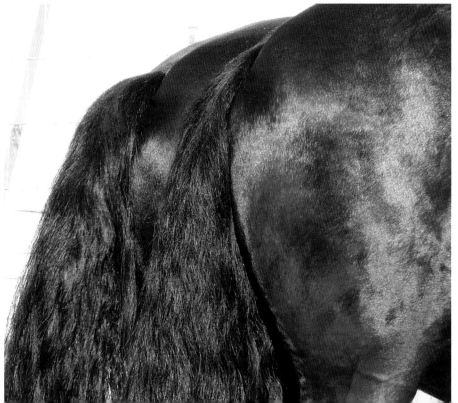

mouth (if we are playing that game). Sometimes I hide it or drop it when he is not looking: it takes him only a few seconds to find it but I have already covered a lot of ground before he gallops after me and hands it to me. He always gets a caress and a thank you.

When I start a number with Phoebus on his own he can be a huge crowd pleaser. We run along together, Phoebus bursting with life and energy. He might jump onto the higher stage level and race along beside and above me. When he rejoins me, I might sink onto one knee and he follows suit; or we run toward the audience and when we reach the low platform that divides the stage from the audience, he lifts his forehand onto it and raises one front leg, pawing the air while the audience applaud. When he doesn't get a laugh he has thought up the idea of baring his teeth or opening his mouth wide. That never fails to get a response. But I don't let him overdo it, so the next moment I drop the whip and run for the exit; he retrieves it and races after me. From one moment to the next, I'm never certain what is going to happen.

I want the horses to be active and animated, I want them to express their pleasure in what we are doing together, each in his own way, but at the same time I have to control their exuberance so that it does not get out of hand. Perhaps a tightrope walker is a better simile than an orchestra conductor!

Overworking

Both Magali and I feel we can sense when a horse is telling us he has had enough. If either of us has doubts about a particular horse, we help each other analyze the situation and come to a decision regarding his involvement. I am sometimes unsure of how hard the horses work in regular, repeated shows, so I have to be extra vigilant. If I really believed I was going too far in any show, I would stop.

Fast Methods

Time, and I mean a *long time*, is so much of the essence of training a horse that any method that delivers extraordinary results in a few minutes—or even hours—is simply not of interest to us. Without any compulsion you can achieve extraordinary things with your horse if you are prepared to be patient and take your time. In so far as it is possible to prove anything at all, we have demonstrated the efficacy of our beliefs by what we can do with our own horses: my liberty acts and Magali's success in competitive dressage. You cannot achieve extraordinary results overnight with our approach, but when you do achieve them, they will be by way of a mutual understanding with the horse rather than simply because you have discovered a way to pass on effective instructions.

The secret of our approach is to build good foundations in preparation for each exercise. For example, when teaching the piaffe, I first touch a young horse in such a way that he collects himself a little bit. I congratulate him each time he does it correctly. Then, when we graduate to the actual piaffe, he can be made to understand that collection is part of the movement; it comes almost naturally if the preparation has been done correctly.

There is no magic formula to achieving a desirable end, like perfect collection. You have to learn and go on learning from your experience. You have to start with each horse as if he were a clean sheet of paper. You have your experience behind you but you must try not to let this experience dictate your approach. You must *watch*. You must be prepared to *change your mind*. You must learn to *listen* to your horse and take into account what he wants to do.

As I've said before, the horse world is often guilty of starting horses too quickly and forcing them at an unnatural pace. The result is that they can be, and often are, burned out at an early age. "Age" musn't be one's guide as to what a horse should be able to do. Mandarin is eight years old and has not yet been used in one of my spectaculars because I do not think he is ready. Templado was never mounted in a show in his life. Bandolero started at five and then continued happily until age nineteen. Dao will be put out to grass soon at twenty-plus.

We hope that in the end you will achieve perfect collection, make a perfect pirouette, or jump the perfect round of fences, if that is your aim, but before you can do this you must learn to enter the mind of your horse, and to open your mind to him. Success is not just a matter of speed and efficiency; it involves an acquired understanding, a deepening of respect that is infinitely rewarding for the horse and for you. For most

Magali collects Bandolero in preparation for the pesade. You can see the exceptional strength of this horse, the good muscle tone, and how his center of gravity is "moved back" to allow for an easy pesade.

of us, to succeed in this quest is a truly life-changing step that inevitably modifies the way in which we treat other people. I personally find I am always looking for and trying to encourage balance and calm in my fellow humans: this I owe to my experience with horses.

A Customer in a Hurry

Once when we were performing in the US I was approached by someone who trained racehorses and had a stable of some hundred horses. He had seen our show and was impressed with our methods and how happy the horses seemed to be. Could I do the same for his horses, he asked, and it was made clear to me that the financial reward for making his horses happy would make it worth my while.

Bandolero gave Frédéric and Magali the idea for one of the Cavalia acts—"Pied Percussion" (literally: "percussive step"). The act was rhythmical, showing off his great strength and energy, and mostly taking place at a canter, with tempi changes, pirouettes, Spanish walk, and ending with a magnificent pesade to the accompaniment of a group of drummers who were dancing with him on stage. All his qualities could be exhibited in this act.

I went to his stable but after a week of observing the methods employed, I had to tell him that it was not possible to achieve what he wanted. All the horses were started too young and pushed too hard. They were mostly finished at five years old and "thrown away." At least this man *wanted* to do everything possible to make the lives of his horses better. There was no lack of goodwill, but in order to move very far in the right direction, the entire system would have had to be changed from the ground up.

Fair's Fair

I talk about rules and it is as important for *us* to obey these rules as it is for the horse to do so. We should know that horses have a real

understanding of fairness or justice. For instance, though it is a golden rule that force or punishment must not be used, it is quite possible to administer a reprimand when a high degree of trust has been established. During liberty training I can tap a horse with my whip on his chest—without him running off—but *only* when he knows that the reprimand was justified.

On one occasion in Brussels, I did a liberty number with Paulus and Phoebus. I had come to think that Phoebus was the "sensitive" brother and Paulus the "colder" one. But on this particular evening, Paulus left me at one point and I was rather too firm in bringing him to order. The next day, I could tell that I had overstepped the mark. I had to be particularly kind and patient with him to make up for it before that evening's performance.

The performance went off well but the experience taught me a lesson: I had misjudged how sensitive Paulus could be. You must constantly be on the lookout for daily changes in a horse's demeanor and never assume that you know a horse so well that you can take anything for granted. Each time you work with him you must adjust your bearings to how you read him on that day. All your knowledge is but a framework on which you paste your emotions, your sensitivity, and those of the horse, at that particular moment. Fortunately, because of the good relationship I had established with Paulus I was able to repair the slight damage in a relatively short time.

Confidence between man and horse is not something that arrives on a plate. And, you cannot just wait about for it passively—you have to work for it. The confidence that I want to have in my horse is about the same as the confidence that the horse will have in me. We both have to earn it.

Dealing with Resistance

Just as it is a natural instinct for a horse to flee from perceived danger so it is for a horse to resist or react to pressure. "Push" a horse with an open hand and he will resist by pushing back. Yank one rein to the side and he will wince with discomfort or pain, and resist. Yank both reins when a young horse is galloping and he will oppose you; he may even gallop faster. Why? Because you have introduced the concept of conflict. A gentle pressure, say that of one finger, or a soft gathering of the reins, producing a feeling only fractionally less agreeable than the state the horse is already in, followed by an immediate release of pressure when he cedes, should produce the result you want.

It is important to remember that the aids we give a horse to transmit our wishes are not natural to them; they have to learn what these aids mean and to carry out the rider's wishes with pleasure. You want to try to make the horse think, "Ah, that's what will restore my previous state of contentment. It's not difficult so I'll do it." If the pressure is violent and painful the horse may well do as you bid but he is doing so because he has "given in." He appears to obey but, like a person surrendering information under torture, he has been cowed and his reactions blunted. You have diminished him with this treatment. The fact that a rider has succeeded in achieving his end is irrelevant; it has done damage and established conflict. People have the misguided idea that you must always "win" every "disagreement" with a horse— but it is not a war. And sometimes you must be prepared to "lose."

Avoid Conflict Even if It Means You "Lose"

The most determined individual can usually "win," and it can be the horse that does so: in fact, sometimes my horse "wins." Faced with an aggressive horse, I might draw back. Whatever happens I must not get into an argument with him. I must not allow myself to be led by the nose—biting, for example, is not permitted—but I must find a way to be firm without fighting. I try to go around a serious problem. I try to find what pleases this particular horse and work out what makes him aggressive. Instead of trying to force him into a state of submission I invite him to cooperate. When a young horse is timid I might try to be less forward and to "shine less brightly."

A "Disagreement"

Magali tells this story: "I mentioned earlier our act where Dao is let loose on the stage and wanders about while I enter on Gracioso, saddled and bridled, and perform various dressage movements. Then I dismount and Fred helps me onto Dao, who has no saddle and just a neckband, and I repeat the movements. Dao loves rolling but it doesn't suit me to let him do so in the dirty grey sand at the beginning of a performance. When we first did this number, Dao thought he would have a roll, but Fred stopped him and made it clear that he didn't want Dao to repeat the attempt. If he had been allowed to have a good long roll, he would have wanted to do so every time we did the act.

"When Dao got up (much sooner than he would have liked) he was not pleased that he had been stopped and set off in a fit of pique, circling the arena once, then twice, and then a third time. Fred and I had to stay calm and not allow ourselves to become anxious even though this was not part of the act. We had to allow him time to reflect, and Dao had to know that he had the right to do this.

"To put it another way, the horse should 'stay with you.' If he leaves for a few moments to let off steam, that is all right. If he leaves and will not return, then he has a reason for it. You have to convince him that it is better to stay with you, although that is not to say he is forbidden to leave.

"Once Dao had thought about it, I could see him slowing down. I called to him with a friendly 'Viens! Viens!' ('Come! Come!') and he did. He looked at me and wanted to know if he was forgiven. I patted him and told him it was okay. From then on he gave an even better performance than usual, and I went through the dressage routine I had demonstrated on Gracioso, but this time bareback and with just a neckband."

Here, Frédéric is training Tabernero for his brother Mathieu, who replaced him in the touring Cavalia show in 2009. While Tabernero has become a good performer, he needs constant reassurance. His ear, turned toward Frédéric, and his general expression show that he is paying close attention. They then pause and relax—the horse is still listening but not thinking about work. Frédéric offers a relaxing and calming hand when Tabernero lies down.

"You Haven't Tamed Me Yet."

In St. Exupery's book, *Le Petit Prince*, the little Prince says to the fox, "Come and play with me, I'm so sad." "I can't play with you," the fox replies. "You haven't tamed me yet." Proper dressage is taming. When you have done it well you can ask your horse to turn and twist, to stop and gallop, to back up and half-pass with imperceptible changes in your weight and pressure in your hands. The horse does not interpret these signals as something to resist. He is tamed, but still free. The Gallop to Freedom!

PRINCIPLE THREE
To reduce stress as well as to become a safe, trusted "haven" for the horse.

Carrot or Safe Haven?

It is assumed by most people that a well-timed carrot or sugar lump is the obvious way of rewarding a horse, winning his trust, and showing your own appreciation. Food rewards can be used to achieve all sorts of results—and have traditionally been used to teach tricks—but do little to overcome the horse's instinct to flee from danger. However, when a

horse suddenly shows some stress, a carrot may distract him from the cause and help him concentrate on what you are doing together. Once when I was working with my two Friesian stallions, Phoebus and Paulus, and they were both sitting facing the audience, one of them was upset by the loud applause and I could see that he was about to get up and leave. A well-timed carrot distracted him and made him forget the noise.

This was a case of a reward altering the focus of his attention away from the source of trouble and back to me. And it succeeded. But normally, what you really want to achieve is this: instead of your horse galloping away from something he does not understand, he stops and turns to you, his accepted leader and friend, because he knows you will understand and explain it to him—indeed that it is better to stay with you than to run off into the unknown.

I once experienced a very striking example of how true this is: the weather was bad and I was in the middle of a liberty act with three stallions when a sudden gust of wind set the sides of the huge tent in which we performed rattling like a theatrical thunder machine. The stallions were at a little distance from me; they stopped dead in their tracks, looked about in alarm, and then came to me for an explanation and solution.

A feeling of security is much more fundamental than the need for food—and so constant, that it is a basic element in the training of a horse. I consider removing anxiety, reassuring the horse, and producing what might be called a "comfort zone," as the steps to be taken before any other. As soon as a horse feels secure you can begin the process of *enabling* him (I purposely don't use the term "making") to cooperate and work for you. My conviction is that the horse has to *want* to work, that he will find pleasure in working, and that the reward he seeks and accepts is security and protection from stress and danger. Naturally, there is nothing wrong with giving the occasional reward, but it should never become an automatic quid pro quo.

I often recompense my horse by allowing him to do a favorite action. As you know, Aetes likes nibbling my chin, so at the end of a show I let him do this and of course the audience loves it. Quite often I will already have left the stage when a horse returns to me and wants to do his favorite thing. If I can afford the time, I let him, and if I don't have time because I have to go on stage again right away, for instance, then I will come back and make it up to him. I have to keep each horse's peculiarities in mind during a show. By remembering to allow Fasto a fair amount of galloping, I reduce his stress. If he is stressed at the end of the act when the horses lie down for the applause, he's tense and shows me his unease. If he has had a good gallop, he is relaxed and sits perfectly still through any amount of clapping.

When Lancelot becomes anxious in the middle of a performance, he is like someone in front of a void: he freezes and his muscles tense up. As soon as I see this, I let him put his head in my elbow, which is his way of telling me that he wants me to calm and relax him.

Flight Is His Right, but My Protection Is Better

The great advantage of liberty training is that there is by definition less stress from the outset. It is often months—with Templado, it was years—before I put a saddle on a young horse. This makes it much easier to encourage, if not to provoke, the horse into showing initiative. I want him to understand that he has various choices even if I help him make his decision. This matter of choice even extends to galloping away from me. Since I am working with him in a closed arena his freedom is, in the end, limited by the fence and he will eventually stop. I may keep his attention by waving my whip or calling softly. I have somehow to convince him that he will not find the peace he wants unless he pleases me and does what I want. Gradually he works his way back to me and we resume where we left off, calmly and without recrimination or punishment. A horse soon learns that the alternative to flight is to put himself under my protection. But flight is *always* his right! It is up to him to decide how to deal with his fear.

Leave Your Troubles at the Office

Magali adds: "It is not uncommon for an owner to take his troubles with him when he goes to the stable for a ride. If a rider is stressed, he may easily have an unnecessarily abrupt reaction to something the horse does. He may throw the saddle on rather fiercely or pull on the reins impatiently. Horses are astonishingly sensitive to this sort of thing and rather than make allowances for the rider they become more tense themselves. All too often a rider has a fixed idea of what he wants to achieve during the session and can exhibit impatience to get on with it. This is a big mistake. You should always weigh your own state of mind and that of the horse.

"It may be better, when you are in a very stressed condition, not to ride at all for the moment; just spend time with the horse, feed him, go for a walk with him, notice what is interesting him and how he reacts to the passing world. You will do your relationship with him far more good than having a stressful ride. After a while, you may see that he has relaxed and that you have as well; then you can let down the stirrups and go for your ride.

"To put it another way, you should try to separate yourself from the day's problems and not have a fixed approach to training. The horse has probably spent the day cooped up in his stall and the last thing he wants or needs is a bad tempered, aggressive rider. He must have the confidence that you are always calm and in control of yourself so that he can trust himself to you whatever the circumstances."

Teaching a Horse to Teach Himself

Teaching is largely a matter of helping the horse to take steps himself, at his own pace and without pressure. In this way he learns to control himself and reflect, to wait instead of fleeing when something unexpected happens. How many times can I say it: time is of the essence. I can spend ten minutes doing nothing at all with a horse except adjusting my breathing to his and massaging him. Calm equals comfort equals happiness. Horses adore being massaged in the right way. The head is an especially privileged place; also, the lobes and base of the ears; the nostrils, gums, and lips; and the base of the tail. There are relatively few places that a horse can massage for himself. Imagine what it would be like to have no arms: how would you deal with a tickle?

When you discover what each horse likes, your gestures and actions bring you both closer together. The horse's growing confidence puts him in the right frame of mind to understand your requests. He "learns how to learn" and that the process is shared pleasure; all activity becomes an enjoyable game that he has with you. There is no need for impatience or compulsion let alone anger. Soon you will only have to present the problem and he will find the solution. It is a very different situation when a horse succumbs to instruction in order to be through with the ordeal, often revealing his submission by his body language, for example, the position of his ears and tail.

PRINCIPLE FOUR
Always to be patient and never push too fast or too insistently—and on the other hand, not to allow the horse to get bored.

Forget Deadlines

Magali says: "In our world everyone is obsessed with deadlines and speed. In the horse's world you have to forget these. If you tug on a carrot, hoping to speed its growth, you will loosen the roots and achieve the opposite effect. If there are difficulties I try to divide them up into manageable parts. I wait until the horse feels ready to take the next step and I am convinced that in the end I save time by this approach.

"When it comes to work I try never to overdo it. Deciding on the correct length of a working session is vitally important. What is more, a horse must feel that if he does really well he will be rewarded with a shorter session. If he is forced to go on too long it not only tires him, it also 'demotivates' him—a great mistake. I try to break up lessons into a logical progression the horse can understand and take pleasure in. When I make a mistake and press him too hard, I can just go back a step without having to go all the way to the beginning."

Trial and Error

The classical teaching methods of horse training are on the whole against experimentation; I believe that trial and error is the only way to proceed because, inevitably, you will make mistakes. As Albert Einstein said, "Anyone who has never made a mistake has never tried anything new." My horse shies: Is that wheelbarrow the reason? I remove it; he shies again. Is it because he doesn't like being away from his friends? I bring them in to the lesson and try again—and so on. I spend my life trying to get to the bottom of enigmas.

Gracil is a very sensitive horse who benefited greatly from Frédéric's patience and Linda Tellington-Jones' help (see p. 51 and also p. 126 for more about Gracil). Frédéric alternates liberty work with work in-hand and basic dressage movements—as they are the basis of all liberty work.

In the sort of acts in which my horses take part they are not made to rear up and hold the position for a long time as they are often asked to do in circuses. I know from what they "tell" me that a long rear is uncomfortable and they don't like it. I once allowed someone to tap my horse on his hindquarters to keep him up. Never again: the next day the horse made it crystal clear that he was upset and didn't want to play with me. The end never justifies the means and in this case, the end was not even the correct one. The horse was able to tell me and I made it up to him.

Some people say that, in a competition, it's all right to push the horse further than he would normally go. My answer is that if you have a good relationship you can ask a lot on one day but the next day you must reward your horse with rest or with games he likes. I usually play a few games before going into the arena and, of course, I choose the ones that my horse particularly likes.

PRINCIPLE FIVE
Never to use force or become angry.

Don't Even Think About It!

As if it were not already obvious, I cannot stress enough that any method based on achieving your will over that of the horse by punishment or brute force is not to be considered. If a horse does not obey you, there is almost certainly a reason for it: either he doesn't understand the command or he is suffering discomfort or pain somewhere, or he is fearful of what might happen if he obeys. Since my aim is to cultivate a relationship in which my horse will *want* to obey me and enjoy doing what I ask of him, I know that a refusal has a reason. It is my job to find that reason and to put it right.

I might add that I was peculiarly fortunate with Templado. Once he had accepted me as his trusted friend he never gave me the slightest reason to be angry but, before he was "tamed," there were plenty of occasions that could have elicited anger had I not been aware that it would serve no purpose.

It seems impossible to hide anger from a horse, and the result of being angry is to seed confusion. I know this because when I was less

ray

ylle

Frédéric on the beach in Paradise Cove with Templado and Fasto, trying not to get his bare feet trodden on! A moment of joy shared by all three of them. They have a rest near the water's edge and then decide what to do next. Another gallop? Why not! Fasto and Templado sit with Frédéric. Horses don't often sit in this position because it isn't something they need to do. Nacarado is an exception to this rule and can sometimes be seen sitting in his stall. At the end of their day off, they walk home along Malibu Beach.

experienced, I occasionally allowed myself to feel upset after a number had gone badly wrong. Even if one does not visibly show displeasure, it seems that horses can sense it, but they cannot make the connection to a deed, and it only makes things worse. They do not know how to cope with our annoyance and conceive it as a form of punishment. As a result it achieves nothing, indeed the opposite from what you intend.

If something is not working out and you have already shown your disapproval without result, it is better to end that particular lesson and come back to it later. If you ever have to use a hard defensive action, say to protect yourself, follow it immediately with an affectionate action. If you correct a horse, do it immediately and then stop. As with a dog, the association of offence and punishment is lost after a very short time. Punishment that is not associated with the offence will only leave long-term resentment and a diminution of trust.

When Horses Remember

Horses do make some associations over a period of time. For example, one day Fasto caused me a lot of trouble and he knew perfectly well what he had done. After the show he hid in the backstage area and we had to go looking for him. When I found him I said nothing and he came up to me, craving affection. The next day he gave a superb performance, and on reflection I decided that the bad behavior had been a result of my not having paid sufficient attention to him on the previous day, the reason being that I had a very inexperienced horse to cope with during the show and had more or less left Fasto to look after himself. I should have realized that he could not have been expected to understand that.

Another long-term connection that horses undoubtedly make is when they are attached to people or another horse. Templado and Fasto were great friends and were stalled next to each other. When Templado went away for a short while, Fasto pined, and when Templado came back he was ecstatic. Since Templado left, never to return, Fasto has not really recovered his spirits.

Magali remembers: "Once and once only I was impatient with Dao during a practice. That evening during the performance he paid me back in spades: he left the stage, forcing his way through the closed curtains that covered the exit. I was left alone in front of an audience of 2,000 people; all I could do was laugh and make a joke of it by shrugging my shoulders. Fortunately the audience understood and laughed with me. After a few minutes someone caught him in the stable and returned him to the stage.

"This demonstrated Dao's quirky quality of being oversensitive about what he thinks is fair, and it taught me a lesson that I have never forgotten. I shall not make the same mistake again. It also shows that horses do remember what they consider unfair treatment."

PRINCIPLE SIX
To establish a more "natural" form of communication—that is, to further new methods.

What's He Thinking?

Books are now appearing that explore the hitherto poorly charted waters of animal-human communication, and such books are no longer treated with ridicule as perhaps they would have been some time ago. There are people who tell of being able to speak to horses or to hear what they are saying. I myself remember many years ago doubting a woman who claimed she could understand what her horse was telling her. Now I feel quite differently. As my understanding has grown I know that I can often pick up exactly what the horse is trying to get across to me and also that I can transmit my own wishes and ideas; I know this because of the horse's reactions.

What Does He Look Like?

Recent studies in human intercourse have concluded that communication between people depends less on the spoken word than might seem apparent. Much of what we transmit to each other is through things apart from the spoken word, in short, body language: the look in our eyes; the movement of our hands; the muscles in our face; our expression; our willingness to listen; and how we respond to the words or actions of the other person. If we are in the sitting position, do we have our legs crossed *away* from the person we are talking to or *toward* them? What are we doing with our hands? Are they relaxed or clenched?

In fact, there are a-thousand-and-one little signs we transmit when we are communicating with someone. And there are many parallels with horses. The muscles on the face are a particular giveaway as to what is going on: a brow furrows, the face appears to contract, the eyes shut slightly, and the chin is tensed. As I have already mentioned, some horses—Guizo, for instance—can have a particular smell on the side of the face when they are tense or when something is wrong.

Use Your Own Skills.

Why do people find it so difficult to accept they can use their own skills—acquired throughout their lives—for dealing with a horse? The problem is partly that when a person is confronted with a horse he often stops *observing* him and instead, falls back on the "knowledge" of past trainers to help him. He tries to conform to this or that method. He has an "end" in mind and, however severe the method, he thinks the end justifies the means. His end is an obedient horse, capable of performing all sorts of maneuvers at his command. As I've said before, my answer is that *the end never justifies the means*. Every step in our relationship with a horse must be achieved within a code of practice that does not permit punishment, cruelty, or compulsion.

Our Body Language

Although we have to learn the art of close observation of horses I believe that they are very sensitive to our body language and behavior. Every movement we make, even the tiniest, is noticed by a horse, and for this reason we must learn to be precise in all our movements and make sure that our thoughts are working in tandem with them. If we make a movement or initiate an intention but our thoughts are elsewhere, the horse can very easily be confused: he is getting two messages and I do not think he knows how to cope with this sort of complexity. It may not have such a strong effect on him as any anger we might express, but it

THE SIX GOLDEN PRINCIPLES OF TRAINING   *175*

is clearly a negative emotion that will harm our relationship with him. Horses that have spent time in the wild are even more sensitive to our every gesture than horses that have been "dulled" by domestic misuse.

What's the Horse Telling Us?

People often ask me: what does it mean when you talk about a horse "telling" you?

There is no clear way of explaining this. You have to be able to "read" your horse and decode his reactions quickly enough to adjust your own actions. I notice that a lot of people do not even understand if a horse is saying "Yes" or "No." Part of your aim must be to arrive at the point where the horse can tell you things, and you can tell him things in reply. Once he has this confidence he will not find it difficult to tell you that he has back pain or that he's tired.

I keep all my senses alert when I am trying to understand what the horse is saying. When I get a feeling I go with it. I sometimes get the strangest images coming into my mind, like that of an open door in a passage. I find that increasingly I can follow my instincts or my instinctive interpretation of images and thoughts. In order to train this ability I sometimes stay close to a horse and observe him while emptying my mind of all other thoughts. I let myself be guided by my instincts. Usually they turn out to be correct.

You may react to this by saying, "How can you prove this?" Here again we are up against the problem of proof in an area where scientific proof is not possible. In my case I achieve things with horses that might not be possible if I were making incorrect interpretations.

There have been people throughout history who were able to ask the most detailed questions of a horse and understand his replies, but this is a very special gift that few people have been privileged to have. My own ability and Magali's is one we have developed over time by the methods outlined in this book. I am convinced that it is a skill available to anyone prepared to devote enough time and patience to its pursuit.

Remember, equitation and horsemanship is not a set art. Our horses are a laboratory where work continues every day. I am always trying new ways to teach them, and that includes making mistakes so that I become conscious of limits.

Listening to Mandarin

Magali concurs: "A little example of what Fred is talking about: when Mandarin was still a young horse and had not yet been mounted, I got on him for the first time. Immediately, I knew that he did not like the unaccustomed feel of my weight so I dismounted. I made a fuss of him and told him that he needn't worry and that I would get off him as long as he found my weight irksome. Some time later I saddled him and, after getting his agreement to have another try, I mounted once more. This time he let me sit for considerably longer before making it clear that he had had enough. And so we proceeded until very soon there was no problem. Mandarin is a strong horse with a will to match—the sort of horse who could easily have bucked if I hadn't listened to him, negotiated with him, and proceeded at the pace that he felt comfortable with.

"It is still a mystery to me why this happens but I find I go through periods—usually lasting a couple of weeks—during which I have such a close, instinctive union with the horses that I know exactly how to react to any situation. I feel particularly serene during these times, and I welcome them because I learn so much and am always at my best with the horses.

"You have to listen to your own intuition; you will make mistakes but these won't be serious as long as you don't persist in the wrong direction. I always advise people not to ask more than three times if not successful. The essential is not to compromise your relationship with the horse. Don't jump an oxer at the price of losing the horse's confidence."

Seeing Words

"People ask me in what form I receive messages from the horses," Magali continues. "I think it works differently with different people, but in my case it takes the form of 'seeing a word.' I suppose actions need a word to describe them, and I will receive a word absolutely clearly on the screen of my mind. I have no doubt at all as to its import. It has happened too often for me to remain skeptical.

"We are in a world where people tend only to believe what they see or experience for themselves. Take the example of flying saucers. I have no idea if they really exist but I am prepared to keep an open mind; if I saw one for myself and was quite sure I had not been dreaming I suppose I would believe in them—but I know that it would be a difficult matter to persuade even my best friends that what I had seen was real. If it is one day proven incontrovertibly that they do exist then the people who were skeptical will turn out to have been as wrong as those who laughed at Jules Verne's fantasies."

There's a Reason for It

Unlike Magali, for my part I tend to "see in images." I try to put myself into the horse's mind and understand what he is feeling and thinking about. When I was a boy my brothers and I spent hours experimenting with trying to send images to each other, and I believe that I have made quite a lot of progress in doing this. For me communication is not a question of magic. A person who has a close communication with a horse can get him to do all sorts of things, but they can be explained. When a horse does something it is partly that he has done it before and partly that the trainer triggers the action, maybe with movements imperceptible to bystanders, combined with the power of his thoughts and intentions. The only magic is that we have not yet been able to describe in physical terms what goes on in the brains of the sender and the receiver.

People Who Claim Special Powers with Horses

I'm always glad to meet people who claim to have special powers with horses, but I'm not certain to be impressed. Much as I try and encourage others to develop their imagination and not to close their mind to what seems impossible, I'm careful of those who claim special powers of insight. On the other hand, I'm convinced that many people have developed what most of us would call "special powers." I don't know how they would describe these or whether they would agree, but I see it as an ability to give out energy and direct it. When I'm with such individuals and in the company of horses, I can feel this energy and the horses can, too. I happened to hear a highly acclaimed young conductor, who had just taken over a leading orchestra, speaking on the radio. He also saw his work with the musicians as involving a transfer and directing of energy.

There are genuinely gifted people and charlatans in every walk of life; one has to be vigilant, but even encounters like the following help to increase understanding.

A woman was once introduced to me as having special powers that allowed her to read the energy level of a horse: she saw the energy in various colors. I knew Guizo was not well at the time and rather miserable, and when I looked at him I had a feeling of something with sharp jagged edges. I took her to see him thinking she might be able to help. After a suitable pause she said, "Ah, I can see that he is a wonderfully contented and happy horse; he radiates green." I then took her to see Gracil, who is not an easy horse, as I've mentioned. She was standing behind him, which I knew would upset him, and when he made his familiar signs of displeasure she said, "Look how easily I make contact with him. See how contented he is."

A Message from Templado

Another time, one of the stable girls told me that a woman wanted to see me; she had an urgent message from Templado, she said. At the time Templado was in the veterinary clinic and had been so ill as a result of kidney damage after his operation that he had nearly died. The girl did not want to let the woman bother me, but I said I would see her.

The woman explained that she herself was amazed at what had happened. Her own horse happened to be in the clinic and his stall was next to Templado's. When she went to see her horse he told her clearly that he was next to a horse that wanted very much to go back to his home so that he could die where he belonged.

This extraordinary news reinforced the message that Magali and I had both received from Templado. He came home and recovered, not only enough to come on tour with us but to perform again for a couple of years. None of us who were there can forget the first time he made an appearance after his illness. The veterinarian who had looked after him was present to make sure that it was not too much for him, and all the staff somehow managed to watch from the wings.

In the stable you would hardly have noticed him, but as the moment for going on stage approached, he seemed to double in size. His neck arched proudly as in his days of glory. He swept on stage and gave the performance of his life. Everyone who knew him, including me, was in tears, and I'm sure no one in the audience would have believed that so recently he had been at the end of his tether.

When he finally gave up performing, he still came on tour with us until one day in Barcelona he made it clear that he did not want to travel any more. This also happened in a strange way: Magali passed him in the stable one evening and got the clear message that he wanted to go home. She hesitated telling me because she knew how much I enjoyed having him with us on tour. However, she did so at breakfast the next morning, where I replied that I had received the same message from Templado at the same time the previous day. Magali's parents came to collect him the next day and took him home.

One of the last photos taken of Templado with Frédéric and Magali.

We visited him regularly, and we could see that in his stable he was happy. Before that he had always pined when left at home while the others went on tour. Thereafter, he was quietly content as if preparing for the end. After a show in Madrid Magali and I knew that he was near to it and had been holding off until we returned. We were both with him when he died two days later.

Transmitting Thoughts

We keep our imagination alive with dreams of ever-closer communication with our horses. I still put my head against my horse's head as I did when I was a child, in case this might aid the transfer of thoughts, either specific ones or perhaps just mood. After all, we have a parallel with this in our own world: when two people are consoling each other for some shared grief or loss, what could be more natural than to embrace and leave our heads in contact for some time? Is this closeness helping perhaps to transfer or share feelings? If one person were only pretending might the other not suspect it? We know so little about things like this and there is very little proper research into these areas, partly because it is not clear how one would even go about it. Normal scientific methods of arriving at proof might be impossible to apply.

We can sense the serenity and tranquility of the herd on the family farm at sunset. It is a pleasure to watch the horses at moments such as these: the hierarchy is established, they have worked out their pecking order, and there is no conflict—only peace.

LESSONS IN HUMAN CONTACT

Our lives are devoted to improving the balance between people and horses by learning to treat horses with the same respect with which one person should treat another person. In doing so we may even improve the way we interact with other people. Indeed a growing understanding of communication with horses can hardly fail to improve our observation and awareness of the feelings of the human beings with whom we have contact. It is to be hoped that this will make us more compassionate and understanding rather than cynical and unforgiving.

WHAT WE HOPE YOU WILL TAKE FROM THIS BOOK

I hope that, at the very minimum, you turn away from these pages with an unshakeable respect for horses and a determination to treat them with consideration. I hope this book also leads to a resolve to gain the horse's confidence; to be honest and open; to try and understand whether the horse likes what you are doing with him; to ask yourself if you are doing something for your convenience or the horse's interest; to channel all instruction through enjoyment; to strive to develop the horse's intelligence and initiative; and to learn to watch and listen, and thereby develop your own powers of observation.

We all fail occasionally when it comes to our dealings with other people, and no doubt we will fail with horses from time to time, as well. But when we do so and let anger or impatience get the better of us, let us make it up to the horse and resolve not to fail again. We all make mistakes and by doing so we discover something about our limitations but, if someone or some horse suffers from these mistakes, then we must do our utmost not to repeat them.

May every rider strive for a better connection with his horse by observation, closer understanding, and patient groundwork. It matters not what discipline is pursued, only that there be a perfectly balanced union between the two—man and horse—so that the two become one.

Fasto in a dream field.

Acknowledgments

We thank our public, who has enabled us to make our dreams a reality. We hope this book will help guide those who would like to join us in our quest.

We thank our families and our friends who have supported us, the photographers who have captured the fleeting moments that make this such a beautiful book to look at, and our horses who have been able to share their joy and their straightforward, honest natures with us.

We thank David who has put into words our discoveries and our beliefs, and lastly our editors, whose trust and support has brought this book to fruition.

Illustration Credits

Frédéric Chehu (pp. 4, 5, 6, 9, 13, 14, 16, 21, 22, 28, 29 *top and bottom*, 30, 31, 34, 35, 36, 37, 42, 53 *left*, 54, 61, 64 *left and top right*, 67, 70, 71, 82, 90, 91, 92, 94, 95, 96 *right top, middle, and bottom*, 98, 100, 104, 105, 110, 111, 112, 114, 121, 124, 126, 129, 136, 137, 139, 143 *left*, 144, 146, 162, 163, 168, 170, 171)

Gabriele Boiselle (pp. 51 *left*, 56, 182)

Linda Alexander-Walton (pp. 2, 63, 64 *bottom right*, 72, 96 *left*, 117 *top right and bottom left*, 132, 147)

Cedric Texier (pp. 156, 157)

Jean Troillet (pp. 20, 53 *right*, 65, 122, 123, 135)

Patrick Domec (pp. 7, 10, 158, 159)

Erick Henry (p. 27)

Françoise Favre (p. 44 *bottom*)

Personal collection of Frédéric Pignon and Magali Delgado (pp. 11, 29 *middle*, 39, 41, 44 *top*, 46, 49, 51 *right*, 52, 57, 60, 74, 75, 76, 78, 79, 81, 83, 84, 85, 87, 89, 104 *top*, 117 *top left and bottom right*, 128, 150, 151, 152, 153, 178, 180)

Watercolors by Frédéric Pignon

"Man has venerated me as a god but treated me as a beast. Take me for what I am, a horse."

—The Horse